Life Chances

Life Chances

A work of sociological fiction

Simon Poulter and Sophie Mellor *(Close and Remote)*,
Nathan Evans, Moestak Hussein,
Akilah Tye Comrie, Trasi, Safiya, Saediya
and the wider community of research volunteers
in Bristol and Cardiff.

Acknowledgements

Written and edited by Simon Poulter and Sophie Mellor (Close and Remote), Nathan Evans, Moestak Hussein, Akilah Tye Comrie, Trasi, Safiya, Saediya and the wider community of research volunteers in Bristol and Cardiff.

Editorial Advisor: Kathryn Castles
Design: Malcolm Garrett and Jane Plüer for Images&Co
Preface: Dr Debbie Watson
Artwork: Close and Remote working with the wider community of research volunteers in Bristol and Cardiff

Life Chances project is a part of Productive Margins: Regulating for Engagement research programme. Research design and delivery has been co-produced between community organisations, community volunteers, artists and academics, exploring life on a low income and the regulatory services that families encounter in two urban settings - Bristol and Cardiff.

Productive Margins Programme Lead: Professor Morag McDermont
Life Chances Project Academic Lead: Dr Debbie Watson

Most community research volunteers are not named as authors to protect their identity and potential implications for individuals.

The programme is funded by the Economic and Social Research Council (ESRC). The programme is a collaboration between University of Bristol, Cardiff University, South Riverside Community Development Centre, Single Parent Action Network (SPAN), Close and Remote and Productive Margins.

This is a work of sociological fiction

Contents

Preface

Life Chances project is an innovative collaboration between University academics, grassroots community organisations and artists and is part of an Economic and Social Research Council (ESRC) funded research programme called Productive Margins headed by Professor Morag McDermont.

Asking questions of how people experience and resist regulatory processes is central to all the Productive Margins projects and they all originated with community organisations working with people at the margins of society asking what questions mattered most to them. In the *Life Chances* project this comprised of the Single Parent Action Network (SPAN) in Bristol working together with South Riverside Community Development Centre (SRCDC) in Cardiff; considering the parents and family members living on low incomes that their services work with and for. Driving questions emerged that focused the academic partners (Universities of Bristol and Cardiff) to consider what the welfare system might look like for families experiencing low income if children and families were truly placed at the centre of concerns?

Such an ambitious aspiration called for innovative ways of working with people. We were keen from the outset to enable participation and engagement from community members but not through traditional approaches of social science research. This was not about capturing 'voices of the poor' – however valid that may be. It was about giving people opportunities to re-imagine their lives, in different systems of regulation using Utopian modes of thinking and expression. To do this they needed to draw upon their experiences and those of people they know. The research team was recruited by members of the communities we were researching with and comprised an academic lead, a researcher and commissioned artists *Close and Remote*. Together the *Life Chances* project has worked across social science and arts and humanities disciplines to draw together methods that engage people at numerous levels; that allow for people to have their stories heard in safe ways; and that provide space for imagination, creativity and future thinking to speak to policy and other stakeholder audiences about everyday people's experiences with societal systems of control and regulation.

Life Chances , the novel, is the product of arts based practice coming together with social science research in co-produced ways, with research 'participants' engaged as community volunteers. Methods utilised have included jewellery making, media and campaign training, poster design, peer learning about regulatory systems, transactional analysis, game design and fictional novel writing. The characters have been developed by people about people's lives and the project process is reflected throughout the novel storylines. This is hugely innovative as a social science methodology as our participants have been co-authors and creatively produced the material for the novel. It is also highly relevant to contemporary policy in the UK as we witness the roll out of the Universal Credit system and anticipate the Government's response to the Brexit vote. What are the likely implications for people's lives as the regulatory systems that currently govern them undergo inevitable scrutiny and change? Whilst we present the outcomes of the project in a fictional, accessible and hopefully enjoyable format, there are serious academic and policy messages that are being conveyed through the real-life scenarios and characters which we hope have an impact on the reader, whoever you may be...

Dr Debbie Watson
Reader Childhood Studies
Academic Lead, *Life Chances* project

Prologue

Ivan Dunhouse-Jones points his finger upwards towards a vanishing point and his dark eyebrows show a strained concern. It's as if he's pointing at something of note in the distance. The assembled scrum of national news photographers snap away. The images are the perfect backdrop for the following days newspaper articles.

The lower floors of the flats behind him are tinned up and full of graffiti. The door entrance panel has been ripped out, leaving a series of exposed cables. Trash and dog mess litters the small grass area to the right of the doorway. The balcony above is scattered with children's toys and a small bicycle. Inside the lobby door, the red painted walls are scuffed and marked from thousands of bodies, belongings and bags scraping along them.

Ivan Dunhouse-Jones turns and sees a man leaning over a balcony, wearing a dressing gown and smoking a cigarette. The man, in his late-fifties, watches the scuffle of media people around the politician.

"What's it like living here?" Dunhouse-Jones shouts over to the man.

"Who the fuck are you?" the man answers back. The press laugh and more photographs are taken.

"I'm Ivan Dunhouse-Jones. I'm a Member of Parliament and I've come to find out about where you live."

"Well, best get back to your cronies and leave us all alone, Mr Dunhouse-Jones. We don't want your kind round here."

"I want to help, sir, it's not right for people to live like this. I've been moved by what I've seen today." Dunhouse-Jones tries to gain a way in.

"I told you, best fuck off back to London, there's nothing you can do here now. We're not zoo animals to be gawked at. You Tory bastards left Liverpool to rot in the 80s and you're no better now."

A young woman comes onto the balcony and tries to tug him back into the flat. He resists and points at Dunhouse-Jones. The cameras click away and the press aid to Dunhouse-Jones moves to end the press call.

"I cannot believe that you have the fucking temerity to come here and stand around in front of those cameras and make out you care. Shame on you, you Tory scum," the man shouts.

The woman pulls him back from the railings. "Come on Dad, leave it now," she says.

"No, Diane, he needs to fucking get out of here," the man says now breathing heavily.

IDJ and his entourage leave the estate. It is 2009 and a few years later he will enter office as Secretary of State for Work and Pensions.

G4N
SECURE AREA
AAA ONLY
DEEP
HOLE

Chapter 1

February

It's still dark as Desiree taps her security pass onto the electronic pad and enters the marble and steel atrium of G4N. She nods a hello to Nathaniel the security guard and makes her way towards the lift.

"You look tired Desiree, you been out partying?" Nathaniel calls out after her. Desiree ignores him, presses the up arrow and steps into the glass sided elevator.

"Kate has left you a to do list in the cleaning cupboard, can you also clean the..." The lift doors shut before Nathaniel can finish his sentence. Desiree mimes that she can't hear him as the lift ascends. What an eediat, thinks Desiree as she steps out of the lift on the 12th floor. He thinks just because he has a uniform he's somehow her boss.

It's almost 6am and she's been up since 4am. One of her Aunty Vee's random, middle of the night phone calls woke her out of a deep sleep. Her Aunty is going through the early stages of dementia and was becoming more and more anxious. Vee was convinced that her children were trying to steal from her and it took Desiree over an hour to calm her down. When Desiree tried to say goodbye by telling her Aunty she had to get ready for work, Vee started on at her asking why she was still doing cleaning when she had a decent education and a first class degree. It was exactly the kind of conversation Desiree could do without, especially at that time of the morning. She didn't want to be cleaning, but after her children's father had left her high and dry, cleaning was the only thing that she could find that just about fitted round school hours. Noah is old enough to get himself and his younger sister Tasha up and off to school in the morning, and then Desiree is able to pick them both up in the afternoon.

Desiree gathers the cleaning materials from the cupboard, screwing up Kate's list after a quick scan. Desiree doesn't know why Kate thinks she needs instructions each day, it isn't exactly rocket science. The office workers make the offices dirty and the cleaners clean them, pretty straight forward. Desiree thinks even someone like Kate could get her head round that one.

After cleaning the offices on the third and fourth floors, Desiree makes her way back down to the basement. In about half an hour the staff will appear and Derek, the main systems operator, will be the only one to say hi.

Scribbled on a post-it note on the secure lower deck doorway are the words 'Deep Hole'. This is where all of the computers are kept and she has been recently instructed to check the air-conditioning units as a part of her regular routine. 'Deep Hole' is the in-house nickname for the super-computer that processes and collates data on Universal Credit claimants. She felt an odd, and momentary, sense of pride when her access pass was upgraded to AAA (access all areas). But then she could pretty much go anywhere in the building anyway. Her mop and bucket act as an invisibility shield – no-one pays much attention to the cleaners. Some superpower, she thinks. Derek quipped that there were only three AAAs in the building including himself – "not even the top brass can get in here, you know!"

She enters the secure area and waits for the three bleeps that are followed by the door control click. She times her morning so she takes her tea break in the lower deck. It's quiet, just her and Deep Hole. She finds the low hum of the computer server soothing. She hasn't told anyone, and she knows it sounds silly, but she feels that Deep Hole must possess some deep human understanding – all those lives fed through the machine, the thousands of gigabytes of data it processes on a daily basis. So sometimes, on her break, she chats to Deep Hole. About her life and her two children, Noah and Tasha. About her worries that another 'episode' is on the way. She knows what people would think if she told them she talked to a computer. She's tried to talk to 'professionals' in the past, but she gets so nervous and her thoughts get so mixed up, it all comes out wrong. And then they just sit there, nodding their heads, writing everything down, doing their 'active listening', rephrasing everything back to her so she ends up unsure what she's said and what they've said. That's what she likes about her chats with Deep Hole. It just listens.

She has noticed a change in Deep Hole, since they uploaded the new 'agile plus' software last week. A sort of intermittent moan has been added to the low hum. It worries her, but she's not sure why. Derek told her that 'agile plus' was yet another version of a software patch that was designed to keep it all working. When she mentioned to Derek that Deep Hole had started making this strange moan, he gave her such an odd look that she had to pretend she was joking.

Desiree leaves the secure area and looks up at the CCTV camera and its flashing red light. She hears footsteps coming down the lower deck stairs and recognises them as Derek's. "Hello, Desiree, how are you?" he asks cheerily.

"I'm ok Derek. I've checked the air-conditioning in the room and it's all fine," she says.

"Ok Desiree, that's great. I hope Deep Hole hasn't been groaning again!"

"No Derek, it hasn't. Though it was cursing you quietly under its breath."

Derek laughs, and clipboard in hand, walks off down between the server racks to start his morning checks.

Desiree has one last look round the lower deck and takes her mop and bucket back out to the lift and up to the second floor.

Diane opens the car door, places her bag on the passenger seat and gets inside. It's almost spring like today but there are still flurries of an easterly wind. She's been up in Bristol for a couple of days now, staying with Kesha in her flat on Ashley Road. Diane and Kesha met whilst they were both at the University of Westminster. Diane stayed on in London after finishing her journalism degree, whilst Kesha went back home to Bristol and straight into a job on the local paper. Diane bounced around various online news sites for a couple of years, writing about anything from Boris Johnson to data dominatrices. Whilst that hadn't given her the stability Kesha had on *The Bristol Echo*, it had given her a lot of contacts and lead her to where she was now, a regular freelancer for *The Image*. With a byline. Not bad for a working-class girl from the Wirral, her dad liked to boast down the pub, on the rare occasions she made it back home. She coped with her dad's tipsy public compliments by reminding herself that he was the main reason she'd been able to get to university. He'd taken any work he could get to save towards her first year's fees, some of it legit, some of it not. After that she still had to work nights and weekends to pay her way. Ended up with a 2.1 and £12,000 of debt. Still it could have been worse, she could be a student right now.

Diane checks her watch – 7.30am. She has spent most of the previous evening framing her pitch for Nick, *The Image*'s political editor. She'd emailed it over to him late last night, and got a mail back saying he'd call her at 7am. She looks over towards the betting shop. An elderly man is standing outside smoking a cigar and greeting passersby, joking and smiling, decked out in a three piece suit, pork-pie hat and cowboy boots. He's there, regular as clockwork, every time Diane comes to visit her friend. Kesha is planning to interview him for her series of 'colourful local characters', along with leather shorts guy and Dutty Ken from the Star and Garter.

Diane starts the car engine, indicates and begins to pull out just as her phone rings. She pulls back in, fumbles in her bag for her phone and sees Nick's name flashing up on the screen.

"Hello, Nick, thanks for getting back to me," she says politely.

"That's ok Diane, but keep it short. I've got five minutes before I need to slide into the editorial meeting. I'll warn you straight away though, budget is tight and I've already over-commissioned for the next two weeks. I've read your pitch but you need to sell it to me," he says.

"Ok, it's about life chances. About different places and people and how there can never be an even playing field. It's about how the political establishment always aim to control the language and by doing so bring their own ideological agendas to bear. It's about real people and how they fail to fit these agendas and then get excluded…and how poverty is actually a construct of the state…"

Nick's attention is drawn to his computer screen as a photo of the recent ex-prime minister aboard Saudi billionaire arms dealer Adnan Khashoggi's yacht, pings into his inbox.

"Diane, I need a bit more than this…I'll be honest I've commissioned loads of these kind of pieces over the last five years, so it needs to be more focused. What's the angle to this piece, why are you interested in it?" he says, occupied by trying to make out who else is visible in the fuzzy long lens shot of the yacht party.

"Ok Nick, here's the hook. Our now Secretary of State for Work and Pensions, Ivan Dunhouse-Jones, went on this tour of Britain in 2009, whilst he was in opposition. He saw with his own eyes what he called Broken Britain and kickstarted a new debate around the family, poverty and making work pay. He realised that if you change the language and use phrases like 'life chances' you can sell a new form of politics to the centre ground based on setting people up on a new path. It has a quasi-religious utopian feel to it Nick, kind of Pilgrims Progress for the second millennium..."

Nick likes Diane's work, she's one of the best freelance investigative journalists they have on the books, but he can't really see anything new in what she's saying. He knows she has an eye on his job. But then so do half the journos sitting in the office behind him. Maybe she's trying to impress the Editor, who's a well known 'frenemy' of Ivan Dunhouse-Jones from way back.

"Why hang a story round old news Diane? Sure the government is set to launch their Life Chances strategy, but IDJ's tour was in 2009, that's seven years ago. Why link those two things together?" He zooms into the photo on his desktop. He's pretty sure that's Ivana Trump standing to the side of the ex-PM.

Diane realises that it's not going well, Nick sounds distracted and uninterested. She needs to up the pitch.

"Ok Nick. To be honest, some of this is personal. The estate where I grew up in The Wirral was one of the stops on IDJ's tour. There was a photo call outside my dads flat. Loads of press photographers and IDJ turning my estate into a circus freak show. My dad had a run in with Dunhouse-Jones, telling him in very plain language how the Tories had shafted Merseyside in the 80s. The right-wing press ran a photo of my dad on the front page, mocking him as a scouse dole queue scrounger. The humiliation hit my dad hard. He's a proud man. He worked hard all his life until he was made redundant at the age of 58." Diane takes a breath, old emotions surfacing.

Nicks attention is fully on Diane. He feels she may be onto to something now. The personal element might just work – 'working class journo goes back to her roots to fight the good fight for her old man' kind of thing.

Diane regains her composure and carries on.

"Anyway. There is a direct line from that tour of 'Broken Britain' to the thinktank Centre for Weasel Logic, which of course you know was set up by Dunhouse-Jones, and the influence they exerted on government policy with their 'Five Pathways to Poverty'. Which leads us onto the current Life Chances Strategy. I want to show the difference between the spin and the reality. What I am proposing is to retread the steps of IDJ and take my own tour of Britain. I've already visited a few of the places that Dunhouse-Jones talks about and looked into it. Of course some of what he says is true but then you read the sub-text and you can see that there are weasel words at play. It's not about giving everyone an equal chance, it's about pushing them into low pay and even more uncertainty than they had before."

Nick decides to go for it. He's under pressure to drive more web traffic. *The Image* is still losing print readers and he's been encouraged by the editor to secure more advertising through online features.

"Ok, Diane, the tour sounds a good way to shape the articles. And I like the personal angle, but lets keep that in the background for awhile. Let that push you forward but not overtake you. Follow in the footsteps of IDJ and knock out some web pieces for me. If it works we can shape it into something for the paper later. I can give you two days research time. Then email me over some treatments…alright?"

"Thanks Nick, it will be worth it I promise you." But Nick has already cut the line.

Sam pads downstairs, picking up Isaiah's discarded school books on the way. A page has been partially torn from Robot Crash 2. He pokes it back in and shouts, "Isaiah, you've gotta start picking up after yourself, there's no reason I should have to do it."

"Ok Dad," Isaiah grunts as he turns over in his bed and pulls the covers tight. "And get yourself outta bed, your Grandma will be here in a minute."

He opens the kitchen blind and stands watching a couple of seagulls fighting over the remnants of a discarded late night kebab. He switches on the radio and starts getting the breakfast ready.

"And that was 'Eton Rifles' by The Jam. A blast from the past and apparently one of the former Prime Minister's favourite tunes. It's 7.59am and you're listening to Panama 101 FM, Bristol's top radio station and its time to go over to the newsroom for this morning's headlines....Over to you Fiona...Thanks Bob. And in the news today. The government have announced the partial roll out of Universal Credit, the new monthly payment for the unemployed and low income workers. We talk to Barry Hamilton, the Chief Executive of G4N, the private firm responsible for administering Universal Credit, about their super computer, nick-named 'Deep Hole' and the software they have developed that they claim will revolutionise the benefit system and, most importantly, save taxpayers money..."

The doorbell rings. Yawning, Sam opens the door to his mother. "Late night?" Ruby tuts as she pinches his cheek. "Mum, come on, don't give me grief, I've been up half the night."

Ruby brushes past him and into the kitchen.

"Are you going to make me a coffee or am I going to have to do it myself?" Sam gets a couple of mugs from the draining board and switches on the kettle. "So why you not sleeping, huh?" Ruby asks.

"I've got that meeting today, with Debra the social worker and Rebecca."

Ruby stirs her coffee and frowns. "Dat girl, what was she doing leaving Isaiah on his own. It's a good job you dumped her. She's no good, no good at all."

"I didn't dump her mum, we agreed to split up. And don't start on at me again about her leaving Isaiah. She made a mistake. She can't afford to lose that job, you know that. They called her in at short notice. She only left him for a couple of hours. He had the telly and some snacks. He is seven years old, he's not a baby. He knows not to play with matches or stick his fingers in the electric socket."

"Chu, but you won't have done dat, would you?"

Ruby gets up and puts some bread in the toaster, and then goes to the bottom of the stairs.

"Isaiah, Isaiah, come give your Grandma a hug."

Sam gets the margarine from the fridge. "No, I wouldn't, but that's not the point. And anyway, I want Isaiah to see his mum. That neighbour of hers has never liked her, what's he doing phoning the social on her? If it wasn't for everything else I'd go round there and let him know exactly what I think of him."

Isaiah comes bounding down the stairs and gives his Grandma a hug.

"How's my boy? You brushed your teeth?" Isaiah struggles to stay still as Ruby straightens his school tie. "Yes Grandma. Can I have jam on my toast?"
Sam hands him a plate of toast and jam. "Right I've got to get off to work. My boss is only letting me have time off for the meeting if I get in early. I had to tell them I had a doctor's appointment. I didn't want them to know, well, you know."

Sam looks at Ruby who purses her mouth and raises her eyebrows in return.

"What meeting?" asks Isaiah.

Ruby ruffles his hair. "Never you mind, pickney. Now you want me to pick him up from school as well?"

"Yes, thanks mum. See you later. Isaiah, don't forget your books." Sam puts on his coat and picks up his bag.

"Yes Dad."

"And eat your breakfast." He calls over his shoulder as he goes out onto the street.

"Yes Dad."

Ruby shuts the door behind Sam. "Right then, I'm going to get me some of that toast and jam as well, then we'll head off."

"Yes Grandma."

After stopping off at Better Foods for breakfast, Diane drives over to Easton, an area of Bristol that is slowly being glazed over by gentrification, with the attendant rise in house prices. She is pleased that Nick's decided to give it a go, but she knows from previous commissions that sometimes things don't get much further than research or even worse, get taken over by another journo with more profile. She has arranged via a community worker she knows to meet with a Somali mother and daughter who have recently arrived in the country. She is wondering if somehow this can be stitched into the life chances research, knowing that it's important to keep it focused, otherwise Nick will blow it out rapidly.

Jamilah, the community worker, appears in the courtyard at the centre. Diane has known Jamilah for a while, ever since she wrote an article on second generation Somalians in the UK.

"How are you Diane, it's been a while," Jamilah smiles her welcome.

"I'm good. Thanks for setting up this meeting, I really appreciate it."

"You need to be careful that you don't push this too hard because she's quite vulnerable. She had a terrible journey from Somalia and I'm not sure she is ready to talk about that yet, to strangers."

"Don't worry, I'll take my lead from you. It's just research at this stage," Diane replies.

Mona and Samira are sitting in the community cafe. Diane estimates that the mother must be around mid-twenties and the child about five years old.

"This is Diane. She works for a national newspaper," Jamilah nods at Mona.

"Hi, I'm Diane, I'm researching an article, thanks for agreeing to meet today," she says. Jamilah attempts to bridge the discussion. "This is Mona and her daughter Samira, they have been in Bristol for about six months, they've come from Italy but they are originally from Somalia. They are staying with a relative of her husbands at the moment."

Mona is feeling nervous and her English is poor. She apologises for her grasp of the language and seems preoccupied with the child. Samira draws some circles on a piece of paper with the handful of colouring pencils that are scattered across the table.

"Do you mind if I ask you a few questions?" Diane asks. Mona looks over at Jamilah, "Waa caadi," and she nods.

Jamilah, who has a healthy cynicism when it comes to journalists, trusts Diane. She wrote a good story on the struggles of the Somalian community in Britain, and treated her interviewees with respect and dignity.

"Everything you tell me will be anonymous," Diane reassures. "I will take notes but I will not include names," she adds.

Jamilah translates as Diane gently asks her questions.

Mona and Samira left Somalia because of the war in the south. Mona has not seen her husband since leaving Somalia and assumes he may have been killed by Al-Shabaab jihadists. She left with nothing taking only her child and the family's savings. They travelled with relatives by car across Ethiopia, Sudan, Egypt to Libya where they paid a trafficker to get them to Italy via boat.

"What was the journey to Italy like?" asks Diane.

Mona shakes her head and starts chatting to her daughter in Somali. Jamilah beckons Diane to the other side of the room.

"I think this story is too hard for her to retell at the moment, especially in front of Samira," Jamilah says. "She had been travelling with her aunt and uncle, Mohammed and Aysha, and her cousins Aldris and Maryam. There were four inflatable boats going to Italy from Libya. They got split up somehow. These traffickers don't care. Her aunt and uncle were in the boat with them, but her cousins Aldris and Maryam were in another boat. Her cousin's boat was the last to leave and was completely overloaded with people. It began to take in water about five hours into the journey and the so-called captain abandoned the boat and joined another one. The remaining three boats just kept going, Mona couldn't make the man driving her boat stop. Everyone in her cousin's boat either drowned or died from hypothermia. Who's to know exactly how they died? It happened in the middle of the ocean in the middle of the night. No-one in authority went to look for survivors. Her aunt and uncle are heart broken. They cannot grieve properly with no bodies to bury."

"Where are her aunt and uncle now?" asks Diane.

"They are still in a refugee camp in Italy. Mona has lost contact with them…" replies Jamilah.

"Do you think I should stop the interview? I don't want to upset Mona or Samira," asks Diane.

"I think you could try a few more questions. Mona is keen to have her story heard, it's just that she doesn't know you." Diane and Jamilah go back to Mona's table.

"Thank you so much for talking to me. I understand it is hard to talk about your journey. Do you mind if I ask you a couple more questions?"

Mona nods.

"How did you get from Italy to the UK?" Diane asks. Mona replies in Somali and Jamilah translates. "She says she had a relative in Bristol and she came in via the port at Dover. But she has no passport and is seeking asylum for herself and her child. She can't tell you how she got in to the UK, she says she paid a Nigerian man her remaining money and he helped bring her in…that is it really…"

Mona continues to talk to Jamilah in Somali. "She can't work in the UK, she has no passport. She has been to the Police and they sent her to the immigration centre. She had enough other documents with her to prove she was from Somalia and they said she has to come back for another interview," Jamilah says.

"Can she tell me what happened at the immigration centre?" asks Diane.

"She showed them her identity card and some pictures she had. They were very official and not unkind but they had a lot of people to deal with, they said. She was interviewed by a woman and another woman was present during the interview to translate," replies Jamilah.

Mona reaches down into her bag. She produces a credit card sized card with her picture on it. Beneath the Home Office logo, Diane reads in bold type 'FORBIDDEN FROM TAKING EMPLOYMENT'.

"So you can't work whilst you are waiting for your asylum claim to be decided?" Diane asks. Mona shakes her head.

"Mona and Samira receive £35.39 each per week from the government to cover food, clothing etc, whilst they are waiting. They are staying with a relative at the moment, but are waiting to be rehoused as they cannot stay with the relative for much longer. Samira is in the school admissions process, but that depends where they are rehoused, they have no choice of where they might live. Mona worked as a teacher in Somalia and what she really needs is help to retrain and to improve her English, and of course the opportunity to work. We have no idea how long it will take for Mona and Samira to get refugee status, it could be one year, two years – who knows," says Jamilah.

"I want to work. Earn money and look after my daughter. She see so much, too much. Too many bad things happen. I want her to be safe. To be happy," Mona smiles at her daughter and smoothes down her hair. Samira holds out a drawing for Diane, a series of concentric circles, with a flower in the middle.

Diane takes the drawing and thanks Samira. She starts to ask another question, but stops mid-sentence. She has, of course, read about the terrible and desperate journeys undertaken by refugees but she has not met someone face-to-face who has gone through it. She can see Mona wants to tell her story but doesn't want to put her through the retelling for no reason. She needs to make sure she can find a way to retell Mona's story before she asks her more. Jamilah and Mona look at her quizzically.

"Er, sorry. May be we should stop there. Thank you so much for taking the time to talk to me today Mona. I would very much like to come back again and talk some more, if you feel up to it."

Mona frowns. "Yes, I can talk more. Maybe when Samira in school?"

"Yes, thank you, that would be great," Diane tucks Samira's drawing into her bag and makes her goodbyes, thanking Jamilah for setting up the meeting.

It's cold but bright outside. Diane takes out her hat and scarf and sits on the bench in the park opposite the community centre. Thinking about the interview, she takes out her notebook and scribbles some notes.

Life Chances

I spent an afternoon interviewing a young Somali mother and her daughter in Bristol. I was struck by her dignity and openness, despite the terrifying ordeal she went through to reach this country. As I start to research and make notes about the state and universal systems, I am left wondering if the sheer complexity of peoples' circumstances is overwhelming us, forcing our political process towards a reactive state. These personal journeys are what I want to write about, how humanity needs to see back into itself and show compassion.

I grew up in Liverpool and was surrounded by working class values. I had few choices and limited control over what was around me but my dad made me go to university - I was the first in our family. That allowed me to step up and see through the clouds and appreciate the unfairness that life deals people. I can see how other people rule now through their privilege, born into it.

These people have become an elite and they can objectively describe the misery of others and convince people that they have the answers. But they've never experienced what I've been through or my family. And they haven't had to flee their country for personal safety like the young woman and child I met today.

I stood on the balcony of my dad's flat where I grew up from the age of five, and watched the media circus that accompanied Ivan Dunhouse-Jones on his famous 2009 tour of 'Broken Britain'. Dunhouse-Jones stood outside our front door pointing over towards the flats on Jason Road. Those flats were where my friends lived and where we played. I still remember my mum calling me in for tea and I never wanted the play to stop. My dad had a go at IDJ on that day, standing on his balcony in his dressing gown, fag in hand. He was then ridiculed and made to look foolish, stupid and poor in the photograph and article that appeared in the *Daily Saliva* the next day. I swore to my dad then that I would do well and I would be in that media pack, and that I would tell the real story and not the manipulated bullshit that papers like the *Saliva* pass off as the truth.

And as for Dunhouse-Jones. You look at his statements and you see a veiled compassion but underneath there is a definite judgemental tone. When I started writing it up, this is what came out:
They have an arrogance and Damascene self-fulfilling logic that actually constructs a parallel network of 'Pathways to Power', that are entwined with the rhetoric surrounding poverty. They make poverty worse. We need to find compassion, all of us.

SHE is sitting in the noise of the G4N Call Centre in the same building where her friend Desiree has 'broken her back' to clean that day. SHE is on Floor 7, surrounded by an array of cheap desks and dividers with 30 other people taking calls. The work is relentless and all incoming calls are recorded 'for training purposes only'. She has to be careful with her words and control her frustrations with her colleagues. SHE kisses her teeth and shakes her head to herself. Demon dem, she thinks. The partial roll out or test of Universal Credit in Bristol has been chaotic and every morning there have been revisions of the call scripts, new e-learning modules to complete. The Key Performance Indicators are getting more and more convoluted. SHE has lost count of all the different targets they need to hit and is fed up with all the changes. SHE just keeps her head down and works, she's tired of playing the game. SHE doesn't socialise with the other call centre workers as she finds them condescending racists. SHE has enough going on with her kids and Shireen's kids, and doesn't have time for Pizza Express outings and late night drinking sessions. And since that run in with Gareth, her co-workers have kept their distance even further.

Michelle the supervisor has been off sick for the last two weeks and in her absence a series of temps from Swansea have been filling in. The latest temp, Stuart, has been trying to introduce some motivational techniques to boost the centre's KPIs. Most of them are pretty lame, and some are downright patronising.

"Right, the phones are going to start ringing in seven minutes people. Remember the four mantras we discussed in last week's rumble. Be happy, be clear, be quick and never escalate to the supervisor, i.e. me, as I've got enough to do keeping tabs on your KPIs," Stuart shouts across the room. "Now, let's see, who is the King or Queen today?" SHE looks up, rolls her eyes and thinks, eediats. She particularly hates this supposedly motivational technique. Being 'King or Queen for the day' was something her kids did in reception class.

Nobody answers.

"Ok, then, erm, what are we singing this morning?" Stuart asks.

"*I Chase the Devil* by Max Romeo and the Upsetters," SHE says. At least on her turn she gets to listen to some decent music. SHE goes over to Stuart's laptop and searches for the track on Spotify.

The deep drum and bass beats out of the tannoy system.

SHE sings as she walks back to her desk:

"I'm gonna send him to outer space, to find another race..."

Asha summons the courage to pick up the phone and call. All of her children, except her youngest, are at school and her husband Abdi is at work. She's been in the UK for eight years now, but the systems keep changing and she isn't sure what she needs to do now Working Tax Credits are ending and the new Universal Credit system is taking over. She's worried her family's income will drop and she's finding it hard enough already to pay the bills. She looks at the clock on the wall again. She's been on hold for almost fifteen minutes now, listening to the same piece of music, occasionally punctuated by warnings about benefit fraud and how "all calls are monitored for training purposes". A voice suddenly cuts into the music.

"Hello, you're through to the Universal Credit Helpline, can I take your name please?" says SHE.

"My name is Asha Silanyo," Asha replies nervously.

"How can I help you today Asha?" replies SHE.

"I'm not sure about this new Universal Credit. Our Working Tax Credit is ending, but I don't know how this new system works." Sabo, Asha's youngest, starts tugging on her mothers sleeve for attention. She pulls Sabo onto her lap and cradles the phone to one ear as she wipes the little girls nose.

"Ok, first you need to get together all of your documents, things like your national insurance number, record of income and your housing circumstances – are you a home owner, private rented or social housing. Then we advise you to go online at *universal-credit.service.gov.uk*. Are you married?" SHE asks.

"Yes I am and we have five children. Four in school and one at home," Asha says.

"Well you can make a joint claim together as a couple. One of you claims online but gives details for both of you. You'll need a username and password to create an account. Plus your bank account details. And you will need to create some security questions, for example where were you born?"

"I was born in Somalia," Asha replies.

"Somalia's a beautiful place I hear. I know these might be very big changes for you, but try not to worry. You need to fill in the details when you create the new account for you and your husband," SHE says.

Sabo wiggles off Asha's lap and starts playing teatime with her dollies. Asha takes the call into the kitchen so she can concentrate. The woman on the other end sounds nice but Asha wishes she could talk to someone she knows, in person. She feels uncomfortable discussing financial matters with a stranger. And how is she going to do all this? She has no computer. Asha frowns and starts to feel the anxiety rising in her chest.

"Once you've created the username and password, you will need an email address or a mobile phone number. And the email address must be confirmed within seven days. Then we can contact you by text or email, whichever you prefer, as we process your application. So, that's it. If you need any further help you can go to your local Jobcentre where they can get you all up online, ok?" SHE reaches the end of the script. Looking at the display on her computer, she can see that call has taken 5 minutes 32 seconds so far. Only another 4 minutes and 23 seconds before she'll need to move onto the next call.

"I don't have an email address or a computer but I do have a mobile number. How long will it take to find out if we can get Universal Credit?" Asha asks.

SHE senses Asha's growing unease. "The system is digital by design and you should have no problems doing this on your mobile phone, or if you prefer on a computer in your local library. We normally expect to process applications in six to eight working weeks but it can take longer depending on your family circumstances. Is there anything else I can help you with?" SHE reads from the script on her computer screen. Her eyes flick from the screen to where Stuart is lounging back on his chair, feet on his desk, smirking at his iPhone.

"My local library has shut down. I'm no good with computers… I can ask my daughter to help me but we don't have a computer or the internet at home," Asha replies.

"We recommend you visit your Jobcentre Plus or you can contact Citizens Advice Bureau where they can advise you on personal money management plans, which you may find useful. " SHE knows she has to end the conversation now, she's reaching the end of the time allocation for this call.

"Ok. But the Jobcentre is so busy and also I'm not claiming Jobseekers Allowance, so can I use the Jobcentre?" Asha asks.

"I can fill in the online form with you over the phone if you are unable to access the internet. You will need to phone us back with all your documents at hand," SHE wishes she could be more helpful.

"But these calls, these 0845 numbers they cost so much money, I was kept waiting for fifteen minutes before I even got to talk to you," Asha replies.

"Yes I know, I am so sorry. I have talked to my bosses about the cost of these calls, but they just say they can do nothing about it." SHE knows she is going off script, but she also knows what it's like to struggle on a tight budget where every penny counts. She frowns at Stuart. Their eyes meet. Stuart takes his feet off the desk and puts his phone back in his pocket.

"Ok, thank you for your help. I will call again," Asha sighs and hangs up.

Stuart signals to SHE to come over. "It's time for your appraisal meeting with Janet."

SHE has been worrying about this all week, she knows Janet is going to talk to her about the incident with Gareth. "Cheer up, it might never happen," Stuart grins as SHE walks towards Janet's office. SHE curses him under breath.

"Ah SHE, come in, come in. Sit down please," Janet smiles at her and starts to shuffle through the papers on her desk. "Right let's get started shall we?"

SHE looks over Janet's shoulder at her reflection in the grime speckled window. Rain runs down the pane, blurring her features. SHE imagines Janet out in the rain, knocking on the window to come in. She giggles to herself and turns her attention back to Janet's nasal drone.

"Here at G4N I like to see us as one big family, one big happy family. And what do families need to stay happy?" Janet looks quizzically, but carries on without waiting for an answer. "They need structure and a clear hierarchy. Mum and Dad at the top and the kids falling in line behind. You have kids don't you? Yes? A partner? No? I guess that's quite common for someone from your, erm, background." Janet tilts her head and smiles, displaying the remnants of a BLT sandwich, the remaining half of which is stashed in her desk drawer, alongside a Cadbury's Creme Egg and an unread copy of *Fifty Shades of Grey*.

SHE can't lose this job, not with Shireen depending on her. She's just going to have to sit and hold it down, take the patronising bullshit she gets from people like Janet every day of the week. She's not going to smile at her though, she's not going to do that. SHE doesn't care if people think she's got 'attitude'. She rolls her eyes at that thought.

"You have food in your teeth," SHE says.

Janet's smile fades as she runs her tongue along her teeth, trying to dislodge some of the lettuce.

Tank god fi dat, SHE thinks, I can't tek looking at that woman's lunch anymore.

"Well yes, let's get back to your supervisor's report, shall we?" Flustered, Janet spills her tea across the paperwork and starts to dab at it with a tissue she pulls from her cardigan sleeve.

"You've scored satisfactorily on most of the sections, but it seems to be Teamwork where you are letting yourself down. I believe there was some sort of incident when someone used the N-word when talking about a paint colour, is that right?" Janet smiles tightly.

"You know you really need to loosen up. That shade of paint did use to be called Nigger Brown. Gareth was just being historically correct. And Michelle, your supervisor, didn't seem to mind, did she?"

No Michelle didn't seem to mind. You damn right, Janet, thinks SHE. Michelle thinks SHE should just keep quiet, just like Michelle does. Michelle thinks SHE will never get anywhere unless she keeps her head down. Yes Sir, Whatever You Say Sir. If you want to be successful as a black person, Michelle says, you've got to play their game.

"...and rappers use the N-word all the time these days, don't they? Eminem, Iggy Azalea, Vanilla Ice…?"

"I don't like rap music," SHE replies, setting her mouth into a rictus grin.

"Oh, I'm sorry. Erm, perhaps you're more of a reggae fan?" smiles Janet.

"Are you a rapper Janet?" This woman cannot be for real, thinks SHE.

"What's your favourite music, Janet? Cliff Richard?"

"Oh I see, you're…look I'm not being racist you know...."

SHE slowly unfolds her hands, smooths down her skirt, and glares directly at Janet. Then unloads, just a little, down onto Janet's carefully sugar frost highlighted hair.

"So Janet, who exactly are you talking to. Me? What do you know about my background, Janet? Really, who do you think you are to make assumptions about how I live my life based on the colour of my skin. I don't know where or when you were told the N-word was ok. Well it's not ok to say Nigger, Janet. It's especially not ok for some white guy like Gareth to say Nigger. And it's not ok for you to say Nigger just because you bought an NWA album when you were younger. It has never been ok to use the N-word. I don't appreciate you telling me about my history, when you don't even know yours. You are a racist Janet. You're a racist because of the language you use, the way you treat people and your lack of listening skills. You sit there doing nothing, puffed up in your white privilege thinking that it is ok to say Nigger now. That somehow all the black men, women and children that have been called Nigger whilst being threatened, violated, insulted and humiliated are just a distant memory, that we've moved on somehow. It just proves that you have no clue or interest. So Janet, it done today. Now. Mi nah tek nuh more of your liberty taking."

"Oh" says Janet, and presses the buzzer under her desk. SHE walks out of the office and into the main call centre. A few heads turn as she begins to sing:

"I'm going to put on an iron shirt and chase the devil out of ert!"

Diane phones Phil from Dragon Welfare, a community support network helping migrants and refugees arriving in Cardiff. Phil is a passionate and dedicated man who has given countless voluntary hours to the network. A recovering alcoholic, he has been dry for ten years and works part time building model boats that he sells on eBay. In the last few months he has done well, selling two models of SS Great Britain and an unusual request for one of The Windrush.

Diane drives over the bridge keeping in the left hand lane. Trucks pass her and the spray makes it difficult to see the road ahead. She can just see the water down below and the mud of the Welsh side. She reaches the toll and fumbles for her credit card and inserts it into the machine. The gate flicks up and a Ford Mondeo aggressively cuts in front of her. She is still thinking about the earlier situation in Bristol. Her eyes flick to Samira's drawing which is poking out of her bag. She cannot imagine what Samira must have gone through.

Phil welcomes Diane to the Dragon Welfare 'hub', as he calls it. It is a tiny room with a smell of damp and piles of boxes creating a wonky maze across the floor. She tries to work out the best route from the doorway to where Phil is holding out a cup of tea, and opts to squeeze past what appears to be a model of the Titanic. The table it's sitting on wobbles as she pushes past, causing the boat to tip over.

"Oh God, sorry Phil," Diane turns and re-rights the model.

"That's ok, love, no harm done. I shouldn't really have these in here," replies Phil.

“Titanic?”

“No, it's RMS Olympic actually. A White Star Line ship, same as the Titanic, but this one didn't sink. Same captain, mind. Sailed before the Titanic, obviously. Anyway, you don't want to listen to me going on about boats do you?”

Diane sits down and takes a sip of tea. She likes Phil. He reminds her of her dad – a working-class man who's struggled with his own demons yet remains open and generous to his community and the changes it's going through. Phil offers Diane a Ginger Nut from the opened packet on his desk.

“You know someone said the other week that I should get an MBE for setting up Dragon Welfare. I had to laugh, didn't I? Can you imagine me hanging that gong round my neck, Diane? I decided I’m going to put something back into the community and I don't need some relic from England's colonial past as a reward, do I?” Phil chomps down on a Ginger Nut for emphasis, and looks directly at Diane. “So, what can I help you with then? What you working on?”

“Well,” Diane replies, getting out her pad and pen. “I'm doing some research for a series of articles retreading the steps of Ivan Dunhouse-Jones's 2009 tour of 'Broken Britain'. Looking behind the governments rhetoric on the causes of poverty, especially in terms of the massive changes to the welfare system with the current roll out of Universal Credit.”

“Oh, yes, I've got plenty of stories I can tell you. With the current refugee crisis we're seeing people from all over the place – Syria, Somali, Libya, Afghanistan, Albania. As well as economic immigrants from EU countries. Some people arrive with literally nothing, whereas others have friends and family already in Cardiff. There's no 'one story fits all' situation. We now run a Wednesday soup cafe down the road in Butetown and an after school club for the kiddies, as well as our English Language classes. You read plenty of stories in the paper about immigrants coming and taking our jobs, but that’s just rubbish. Those waiting for asylum aren’t allowed to work, and most want to I can tell you. And the other immigrants, people who can legally work, well they’re not taking jobs off local people, they’re mostly doing the jobs local people don’t want to do. And who knows what will happen with Brexit? But I have been bowled over by the generosity of the people of Cardiff. When we made a call out for food I literally had more tins of food than I could cope with,” he points to the boxes.

"So, it's more complex than just benefits and welfare?" Diane asks.

"Oh, yes of course. You're dealing with real people every day in crisis. Some of them have temporary housing, no income and children with special needs. Not to mention the violent and abusive situations they have left behind in their home countries, plus the unspeakable journeys they have undertaken to get here," Phil replies.

"What kind of things are they dealing with?"

"Well if I was to pick one thing out it would be the fact that the system bounces people from pillar to post with no real understanding of the impact of all of this. I had one lady in here the other day with no passport and no records. So she can't really move past go with that situation and she's got two little ones to look after," says Phil.

Diane writes everything down in short hand. She imagines the pitch back to Nick as including the plight of migrants and refugees entering the system. She really wants to make an impact. She's worked hard to get onto *The Image*'s books as a freelancer, but she wants more security. A permanent position with prospects would be good, something like Nick's job for example...

"I'm going to take you down the road to Northside Community Centre and introduce you to Jonathan, the community support worker there. He's a lovely boy, studied Social Policy at Cardiff Uni and decided to stay on here after he finished his course," says Phil.

On the way to the car she sees black bags of rubbish piled up in a small front garden. There is a smell of rotting food and children's toys cascade out onto the pavement. They get back into Diane's car. The rain is now sleeting across the street and buses pass by splashing the few people walking towards the city centre.

They arrive at Northside and Phil presses the buzzer. At the reception Jonathan greets both of them and says hello to Phil in Welsh. Jonathan is a tall man in his mid-twenties who works out regularly at the local gym. Diane tries to establish his ethnicity but can't be sure. Jonathan takes them for a tour round the centre. There is a creche, computer room and a large office for the workers. The workers all look up and greet Phil and say hello to Diane. Through a security glass window, Diane sees a group of women sitting at desks, most of them wearing hijab.

"They're learning English," Phil explains.

"I'm going to introduce you to Najma, who is one of our clients. She has come to Wales from North Africa. She is happy to speak with you on the basis of anonymity. I think you'll be surprised, hopefully in a positive way," says Jonathan.

They enter a small room and sit down. Najma smiles at Jonathan and Phil. Jonathan introduces everyone and then asks if they want a drink. Diane asks for tea and Phil requests Diet Coke. Najma asks for water.

Diane looks over to Phil to break the ice.

"Diane is writing an article for a national paper about the benefits system and she wants to speak to a range of people. Is it ok if she asks you some questions?" says Phil.

"Yes of course," says Najma.

"Well, it's kind of changed a bit already, I've met a few people and I can already see it's much more complex than I thought..." Diane tails off.

Jonathan returns with the drinks and sits down. He talks about the importance of anonymity and reassures Najma that people in Wales and Britain need to understand what is really going on.

"Can you tell me about how you came to the UK, please?" asks Diane.

"I came with my daughter, she is nine years old. My husband had a job in insurance and I worked as a doctor. It became very dangerous where we lived in North Africa, there was war. I was scared for my daughter. She kept telling me she was unhappy. She stopped going to school. There were armed men everywhere and I stopped my work as a doctor, everything was breaking down. We had no water and days with no electricity. I have British citizenship. I decided to leave North Africa for UK for my daughter, to keep her safe. My husband did not want to leave, he is there still," Najma stops abruptly and looks down.

Diane can see that Najma is distressed talking about her life in North Africa and wonders if they should carry on with the interview.

"Can you describe what it was like coming to the UK?" Diane asks.

"Yes. We have moved twice from other cities and now we are here in Cardiff. My daughter goes to school and she is doing well. I am improving my English as well and trying to work. I want to be a doctor again but I need to pass the exams. I need money to do this but I spent all the savings I had during the first six months in the country when I was not allowed to work or claim benefits," she says.

Jonathan explains that Najma needs an average score of 7.5 in the International English Language Test. This costs £900 to take. If you fail, you have to pay the same fee over again to retake it. She needs this to then go on to take the Professional and Linguistics Assessments Board (PLAB) test which tests clinical and language skills.

"The PLAB comes in two parts and costs £1,070 and you can only take it at registered centres. This makes it very difficult for me. I am a single parent. It is also hard to find opportunities to get clinical experience in Cardiff," Najma tells Diane.

Diane tries to guess how old Najma is, maybe mid-thirties? She also wonders how much pressing she could do in the interview. She knows that this personal story would be fabulous for an online piece because it challenges many of the preconceptions around refugees and migrants. She decides to push it a bit further.

"Can you tell me what the system is like in more detail and what you'd like to happen for yourself and your daughter?" Diane asks.

"I want my daughter to be safe and I want somewhere to live. I want to work and I need to look after my daughter. I have to do the English tests, some of them in London, if I have the money. I need clinical experience in this country but you can no longer volunteer to do this because of regulations. I want to make my life again and to help other people," she says.

"You can see the problem, can't you Diane? Migrants come to this country with skills that this country needs, but they are prevented from using those skills by bureaucracy and financial barriers," Jonathan interjects.

"Najma, would you be okay if I did an online piece about you for the paper? Of course you wouldn't be identified." Diane asks.

"Yes, I can meet you again for an interview," Najma replies. "There are so many negative stories in the papers about immigrants. But please, it must be anonymous. My daughter, she must be protected," she says.

Diane thanks Najma for her time and asks her for her mobile number. Najma writes it down on Diane's notebook. "Ok, I'll be in touch," she says.

Jonathan shows Phil and Diane out to the reception area. It's now raining heavily. Phil zips up his parka and makes a dash for the bus, calling out a "goodbye" and "stay in touch" over his shoulder. Diane crosses over the road to the car park. She jumps back in the car and drives through central Cardiff towards the M4 motorway.

Sam and Rebecca sit in silence in the meeting room, waiting for their social worker Debra to arrive. Rebecca sits slouched in her chair playing Candy Crush on her phone. She doesn't want to be there and she certainly doesn't want to spend any time with Sam. She can feel the blame coming from him in waves. At least he didn't bring his mum. She couldn't have coped with that pursed-lipped busy-body preaching at her. She'd had enough of that when she and Sam had been together. She could never do anything right in that woman's eyes.

Debra enters the room and asks them if they need any water or anything. "No," says Sam. Rebecca doesn't say anything.

Debra sits down and searches for the correct file in her cavernous bag. She looks for her glasses and then remembers they are on her head. "Rebecca, sorry, could I just ask you to put your phone away, just whilst we're talking?" Debra smiles and nods at Rebecca. Rebecca slips her phone in her pocket and sits frowning at Debra, arms crossed. Great, another middle-aged busy-body telling her what to do.

"Right, now. The purpose of this meeting is to establish what happened with Isaiah being left on his own and how he can be cared for in the future," Debra says.

"I'm here to work with you both to put together an action plan for the next few months. We will then review this and see how things are, does that all make sense?"

"Yes," says Sam, flicking a look at Rebecca. Again Rebecca says nothing. Let him glare, she thinks. She's not going to make this any easier for him, with his disapproving glances, and holier-than-thou attitude.

"My job is to make sure that Isaiah is safe and well-cared for, so to do that I want help from you both. Does that seem fair?" asks Debra.

"I don't trust you people, you seem all nice but really you're just trying to trip me up. I know what you're like and how you operate," Rebecca says, feeling anger building inside her.

"So, you feel that we may appear to be nice but really we're not, is that right?" says Debra.

"Yes, what I feel right now is anger towards all of you, towards Sam, Sam's mum and the Police," Rebecca says.

"So, you feel anger towards everyone and that must be difficult for you to deal with?" says Debra.

"Yes, you people… you've pulled my life apart and now you're just sitting there and repeating back at me what I'm saying. I have every right to be angry. Just one mistake and I can't see my boy. And I know it's because of my background. It's not my fault my parents couldn't cope. Don't blame the children for the parents' mistakes. That's not what's happening with me and my boy. Just because I was in care doesn't mean I don't know how to be a mother," Rebecca says now leaning across the table at Debra.

Sam sighs. "I want Isaiah to be happy and to get on at school. He's missed Rebecca the last two weeks and he needs to see his mum. I want that to be arranged next week."

"We have to make a decision now around visits and how both of you can work together in a positive way. What I want to suggest is that Rebecca comes over to your house Sam, or to your local park, for a supervised visit early next week after school. How does that sound?" Debra suggests.

"Yes, we can do that," says Sam.

"Great. We have carried out a risk assessment and will be continuing to look at risk. I am happy that you both want to find a way forward for Isaiah but I am acknowledging that for you Rebecca there is still some concern about how we work." Debra feels the room is getting very tense.

Rebecca looks at Sam. "Once we've gotten through all this I want Isaiah living with me. Ok. I'm the mum. He should be living with me," she says, holding back the tears.

Sam starts to feel angry, he doesn't want to do this in front of a social worker.

"Look, we agreed Isaiah would live with me. You're the one who left, you're the one who said they couldn't cope. You can't just take him, his home is with me," Sam tries to keep it down, but Rebecca knows how to wind him up.

"That was over four years ago! Things have changed. I'm settled now, I've got my own place and a job. I only made one mistake and I only did that because I wanted to prove to you and your mum that I can cope, that I don't need to rely on anyone else," Sam can see tears starting to well up in Rebecca's eyes.

Debra interjects. "I can see that you're very upset Rebecca. I want to assure you that we are going to work together to look after Isaiah and of course during that process make sure that you and Sam come to an agreement."

"You're just trying to take everything away from me. I was really beginning to get my life sorted." Rebecca wipes away her tears with the back of her hand and gets up.

"It's just fucking white people telling us how to live our lives all the time. And you Sam, you're just as bad, towing the line. 'Yes m'am, no m'am, of course I'll eat shit, m'am'. He's my child and I want him back." Rebecca shouts and storms out of the room.

Sam watches Debra writing in the file.

"We have to write notes of the interviews, to keep on file, it's just a procedure," Debra smiles. "I suggest we find another date in March and in the meantime I'm going to write to you both and we will organise a supervised visit after school on Tuesday."

"Ok, thank you," says Sam and gets up to leave. "She doesn't mean all that, she's just upset."

"Yes, yes, I know. But it would help if she tried to work with us, just a bit more." Debra replies.

Sam replies with a tight grimace and walks through the doorway. He doesn't want to be here, having strangers telling him how to bring up his child. Rebecca shouldn't have left Isaiah on his own, but he's pretty sure if they were a middle class white family living in Clifton, none of them would be here right now. Rebecca is a good mum, he knows that. And he just wants Isaiah to be ok.

Debra finishes writing up her report, noting that the mother has considerable antagonism towards social services and recommends that she attends some anger management classes and has some counselling sessions with a psychologist.

Chapter 2

March

Diane is back in London at *The Image*'s office near King's Cross. After a meeting with Nick earlier in the day she has now got a commission to write six online pieces during her tour round Britain. Nick liked the migrant angle and gave her a strong steer to open up the 'cross currents of migration, benefits and real lives'. She is pleased that he's gone for it and now needs to plan the whole process out. The bit that clinched it was the idea of following the trail of Ivan Dunhouse-Jones. She talked to Nick about arranging a meeting with IDJ to give it some tension and balance. Nick thought that she wouldn't get anywhere near him, as he knew that the minister didn't care for 'liberal lefty journos' and *The Image* had run some unfavourable articles on the problems with the IT procurement for Universal Credit.

Undaunted, Diane manages to get a number from one of Nick's colleagues for IDJ's personal assistant.

"Hello, this is Diane Butler from *The Image*. I'm writing a piece on poverty and I wanted to do an interview with IDJ on his views and experiences. In particular his tour of the UK in 2009. It's going to be an online series of interviews and pictures..." says Diane.

"Let me stop you there. I'm afraid Mr Dunhouse-Jones is not doing any media work in the near future as the PM has asked him to draw up plans for the coming election in October. He will be happy to give you a written statement of course," replies the PA.

Diane ends the call and feels deflated that she can't get an interview. She decides to give it another try when she's got some interviews and travel under her belt. She writes some more notes.

Life Chances

I've started looking into the background of this phrase 'life chances'. I literally spat out my tea when I discovered that it connects back to a sociologist called Weber and he in turn connects back to Karl Marx. So how did the Tories land on that one then?

Weber talks about 'status groups' - a way of talking about social classification. That answered it for me really. The Tories love to place people in categories. Reading on, Weber talks about how people acquire status and influence, which links to things around them. When I got back to Liverpool from Uni, I realised that I had changed. I had expanded my worldview and saw things differently. Of course these 'status groups' influence public opinion and shift the political process. It's obvious really that Weber's writing is the juice of the current media machine and the manufacture of points of view. I talked to my dad about this and he agreed. But then as Dad said, it's not always that cut and dried. Just look at Hillsborough and The Sun. Liverpudlians still do not buy The Sun twenty-eight years after their inflammatory headline 'The Truth' screamed that drunken fans had pick-pocketed the dead and fought valiant police as they tried to help at the Hillsborough football stadium disaster.

The question is how do people in real situations of struggle acquire the same tools of representation and power as the political elite and the media? This is what I am going to write about. I am going to find out if this can be done.

Marx talks about communal action. What I'm hearing now is that nobody wants to have a go for fear of losing their job. Dunhouse-Jones has his Centre for Weasel Logic. This 'think tank' now systematically constructs policy ideas and thinking for the government - my question is who does it for the real people?

How does the system return to the idea of helping people with complex problems, rather than sitting in judgment over them?

Diane walks over to the water cooler in *The Image* hot desk space. She meets Cassandra. "Heh Diane, I've got a great piece of gossip for you," she says.

Toby Thomas ping tests a new piece of infrastructure for 'Deep Hole'. He spends his weekends in his loft apartment near London Bridge tinkering with computers and playing hacking tricks with people on the dark net. He jokes to his mates that he can create them a Universal Credit identity with a few shell commands on his Linux box and if they're lucky they'll receive a direct deposit in six to eight working weeks. If they're not lucky, they will have to do it old school, by hand. Then wait three months and still get screwed over. "Just like #reallife, bruv!" he quips over chatbot, adding a couple of 'laughing cat' emoji's for emphasis. On the wall of his hack studio he has a logo of a well known world bank butting up to an 'Anonymous' Guy Fawkes mask. It's to remind him that good hackers face both ways.

"Just imagine it," he types online, "we can make credit universal to anyone that wants some! Ha, ha, LOL..."

He further boasts that he's been asked to stage an attack on the system using denial of service tactics and invites them to join in the mayhem. Over the weekend, they bring the system down to a crawling trickle of data before laying off and heading over to take on some 'blackhats' in a far flung corner of the web.

On Monday morning Toby crawls into work with a major hangover to be greeted by Barry Hamilton's personal assistant Jane.

"Toby, Barry wants a word..." she says.

From Barry's office there is a stunning view of the Thames. A large telescope is situated in the corner and an oak cabinet full of silverware for 'successful service to the services industry'. Barry's desk is constructed from recycled plastic containers, a hallmark of G4N's commitment to 'Not Just Serve but Save the Planet'.

Toby walks in casually. He has established an unusual relationship with Barry, unlike any other of the 7,500 employees in the IT consulting group of G4N. From a hire as a Junior Systems Operator he has risen to IT Senior Vice Principal at G4N in under five years. Throughout his time at the company he has steadily built up a reputation for getting 'under the hood' of big IT projects and fixing failing government schemes that have come in from elsewhere.

Toby has saved G4N around £2million with his highly creative coding, and he knows it. This fact, coupled with his natural born distrust of authority, has given Toby licence to annoy his superiors on a regular basis. But he gets the job done, and more. Which is something Barry has to remember when Toby is being particularly obnoxious. Barry, of course, knows exactly how to work Toby's father/son complex, with Toby practically rolling over for a tummy tickle if Barry lathers on the praise.

"Toby, I want to congratulate you on the denial of service testing over the weekend. We can now demonstrate back to government that through our agile approach we are learning and evolving a truly robust system that can cope under any circumstances. If you could convey my thanks to your team of 'angels'. Without them we would not be the leading service design company in the UK. Remarkable, Toby, you've really impressed me and the board."

A light blush covers Toby's face, and he starts to fiddle with the objects on Barry's desk to disguise his pleasure at Barry's words.

"And now I have something very important to discuss with you. Coffee?" asks Barry.

"No thanks Barry, I had a Jbomb on the way up here," replies Toby, picking up a framed photo of Barry shaking hands with Donald Trump.

"That's some hairdo, huh?" Toby jokes.

Barry takes the photo frame from Toby and replaces it on his desk.

"No calls or interruptions for the next ten minutes, thank you Jane," he calls through the doorway and then shuts the door.

Barry walks towards the Thames view and, as if in a cheap sixties movie, clasps his hands behind his back and then turns to face Toby.

"Toby, Deep Hole is now approaching £16 billion in overall cost. I've had a few emails from the Secretary of State's office and following the recent Freedom of Information requests from Welfare Action, the government are likely to have to reveal the arse end of this whole fairground ride to the baying masses. Hopefully the courts will help out and they have some excellent lawyers in place to stall things for quite a while. I need you to use this time to take on the 'clean up' role with your angels – basically you have carte blanche to look the whole thing over from top to bottom. Report back to me in two weeks' time. What I want is a 'reveal: conceal' analysis, similar to the work you did on the NHS databases last year. I need to go back to the Secretary of State with a position that convinces them to continue with full roll out for completion next year. I need not tell you that you and the angels need to do as much as you can off the books."

As usual, Toby has few words. "Ok chief, leave it with me."

Toby walks out of the office, winking at Jane as he passes her desk. He pulls his Android phone out of his hoody and over his PGP encrypted email he pings off a group message to his angels.

'...STAND BY YOUR BEDS ANGELS, PREPARE FOR PIZZA – lithium...'

Jane and her admin team watch Toby swagger towards the lift and press his thumb on the restricted access pad. They have heard via Radar about the 'orange floor' in the annex. Pink sofas, sauna room and full black out windows, along with all night parties and open accounts for take away. Rumour has it Toby and his staff hacked the human resources database and emailed a G4N salary chart round the building showing Toby and his fifteen colleagues to be the highest earners alongside Barry Hamilton.

A new face exits the lift just as Toby is entering. Barry pops his head out of his office and shouts across the floor. "Hi Jem, good to see you. Toby, hang on a minute, come and meet Jem."

Barry introduces Jem to Toby as an old friend from Dragon School, which makes Toby smirk. "Is that some kind of Harry Potter thing?" he asks with a grin.

"No Toby, it's a prep school in Oxford," Barry replies, "for someone so intelligent, you do, occasionally, sound like a prat."

Toby knows he irritates the hell out of Barry on a regular basis, but that Barry needs to keep him, the coding cash cow, sweet. Toby folds his arms and mutters, "whatevs," as he shrugs.

"Jem is a communications special adviser at the DWP and will be available to us, Toby, for this period. I'd like you to report to him as well as me, for the duration. Jem, Toby is in our gifted and talented team on the orange floor and has done some fabulous work for us over the years. Ok, thanks Toby, I'll see you later?"

Toby gives a mock salute and returns to the lift. He doesn't like the feeling that he has just been dismissed by the Headmaster. And he doesn't need another silver-spooned pinstriped a-hole hovering over him. He wanders what you call a pair of public school boys. A double Johnson? And what about a whole group of them? A bollock sack of Bullingdons? He gets out the lift on the orange floor and logs onto http://CONspiracy.com for a bit of idle surfing.

Barry closes the door to his office and wastes an hour being patronised by Jem telling him things he already knows. He doesn't want Jem there, but he's been foisted on him by the ministry. A couple of years younger than Barry, Jem had been Barry's 'fag' at public school. Jem had been a snivelling little toady boy and had grown into a conniving and slick adult. Perfect for a parliamentary special advisor. Now Jem seemed to be taking delight in having some sort of power over Barry.

It made Barry cringe, but he'll put up with Jem's little power trip for now. Governments change. Business, on the whole, stays the same. He would outlast Jem, that's for sure.

Later they emerge and take a taxi over to Caxton House to meet with a team of senior civil servants. On the short taxi ride they discuss the main issues with Deep Hole and Universal Credit, agreeing that the communications have to remain positive and constant while things get sorted out.

Barry and Jem are ushered into a wood panelled meeting room. A long oak table runs the length of the room. A portrait of Margaret Thatcher looms down from the wall at the head of the table, and a digital screen faces her from the opposite wall. Bottles of sparkling mineral water punctuate the table at precise intervals. Each place at the table has a copy of the report Barry had prepared earlier. He walks with confidence towards the screen, hands a USB stick to a waiting PA and starts his Powerpoint presentation.

The impassive faces of the gathered civil servants slowly become animated, nodding and some even smiling as he goes through his slides. He ends with a diagram of the Deep Hole network.

"You see we tend to think of large computer systems as occupying a James Bond like dark basement. Actually, we do have one of those at our offices, but in truth Deep Hole is everywhere. It is a growing network of data centres based both in the UK and overseas. And as it grows, Deep Hole will become the over-arching system and network that governs our lives as a part of gov.uk. It will hold more data than any other previous system, it is 'digital by design' and will ultimately process millions upon millions of claims and it will reinvent the way we do work and what we used to call 'welfare'. Of course there have been a few teething issues, like with any new process, but it will reduce our ageing system of benefits offices to a click of a few buttons. A modern miracle. And of course our job now is to bring this to you in an efficient and timely manner, perhaps acknowledging that where other companies have failed we have been able to bring the added value of G4N to bear. We design the best services at the best price. Thank you."

A round of applause follows.

"Any questions?" Barry asks feeling elated that he has pulled one out of the bag, with a potentially negative group of people now smiling. He looks across at Jem, who nods back at him in a particularly condescending manner.

“What is digital by design, Mr Hamilton?” asks a woman seated next to Jem.

“Excellent question as usual, Sarah. Digital by design means that the full roll out is focussed on a top to bottom digital service from applicant to database and assessment back to payment or refusal. No paper in sight, cleaner and greener...”

“But what about applicants with low level digital literacy or no access to computers?” she responds.

“Another fabulous question. Of course our role is on the digital and data management side but I am aware that measures are in place to take in applications over the phone,” Barry answers.

“What about assessment and letting people know what they can get?” asks another voice.

“Well that’s a question you chaps at the DWP are best suited to answer. But we currently have the system up and running with an indicative amount on the final screen. That leaves the applicant with a good sense of where they are.”

“I’ve heard that there are issues with claimants getting into debt because they haven’t been paid quickly enough, how does your computer handle that Mr Hamilton?” asks a man at the far end of the table.

“I am sorry but that question is beyond my brief, again that is something for the DWP to look into. At G4N we specialise in providing agile and integrated computer systems that can work with real time data. How that system is then administered is up the the client.”

“The system is built around the client having a bank account. But what if they don’t?” probes the same man.

“Whether we like it or not, we are now living in the digital age. This system is digital by design. The payments are electronic, so you must have a bank account that can accept electronic payments, it’s as simple as that.” Barry retorts, feeling exasperated.

Barry looks at his watch. “Well I think I have taken up enough of your valuable time, ladies and gentlemen. You'll find a full briefing in the pack in front of you. If you have any further questions, please don't hesitate to contact my office and I will be only too pleased to answer them personally."

Barry retrieves his USB stick and nods at Jem.

"Now I promised I'd pop in and see IDJ whilst in Westminster, and, as I'm sure you are all aware, IDJ is a creature of habit, so if I head off now I know I'll find him in the Pugin Room with his morning coffee and croissant." A polite ripple of laughter follows Barry and Jem as they leave the meeting room.

Out on the street, Barry lets his annoyance show. "God I hate government mandarins. Those smug bastards think they run the country."

"Yes, and that's why you need to keep them on side," replies Jem, hailing a black cab.

"You need to keep on message whilst you iron out the glitches. Whilst I concede that you inherited a compromised system, we're paying you big bucks to sort it out fast. The election is looming and we don't want the opposition to get their grubby mitts on what's really happening with Deep Hole. I suggest you get Toby on it asap. Let's see if he is as good as you say he is."

God, he is a pompous little twerp, thinks Barry as he checks his iPhone for messages.

Jem gets into the cab and calls through the open window as it pulls away, "I'll see you back at the office. Enjoy your beano with Dunhouse-Jones and give the old Buller a wedgie from me for old times sake, eh?"

"Oh yes, ha ha," Barry mutters under his breath as he watches Jem depart. "I seem to remember it was Dunhouse-Jones who was giving you the wedgies whilst we were at Brasenose, you twat."

SHE walks down Albion Road and knocks on number 23.

"Noah me sey turn the telly down and Tasha stop teasing your brother," Desiree comes to the door, looking harassed. "Come in, come in. I'm just putting the shopping away,"

Desiree smiles at her friend. SHE walks into the kitchen. There are shopping bags on the table, and the kettle is whistling on the stove. She gets the herbal teabags out of the cupboard and Desiree hands her a couple of mugs.

SHE can't wait for the usual 'ah, wha, gwaan, how are the pickney dem,' and goes straight in.

"Ah, I'm free, I told you I would do it. Mi tell dem fe keep dem tings, dutty jankrow dem. I'm just tired of playing the game. Imagine de supervisor talking to me suh, she bright. So I just had to gi it to ar. I feel soo happy I can't even talk, my girl. They've worked me for nearly two years and not one day did I enjoy it. The only person to consistently reach targets was me but yet I was never recognised or shown appreciation, even a dog they would give a bone to. All Mary get 'certificit' fi reach her targets once every six months. Now it's my time, I'm going to change my life." SHE stirs her tea, takes a sip and sits back.

"Lie! Ah what a sintin dat!" Desiree shakes her head in disbelief, "ah wha you go do now? Weh you ah guh do fi money? Hey me here seh you can't get any money if you quit, missus. Rent need fi pay? You have a good wage at that job, yes?"

"I tell you what I got, I got stress and pressure every day for seven hours a day for minimum wage. Demons. I gave my best, they received my best and I received disrespect and disregard. I watched as other people got bonuses that I was entitled to but never received. I got to follow a script and give constantly changing and contradictory information that I didn't agree with. I felt like a hypocrite. Like I sold my soul. Imagine I could only signpost to other voluntary advice services that I knew were unable to help or support them in the way that they needed," SHE kisses her teeth.

"I felt so embarrassed being forced to treat people as if they were less than human. You weren't allowed to speak to the same caller more than once. I mean how backward is that, it's common sense that less time would be taken up if contact had already been made. Faceless, totally faceless. Well, no more. Done it done. Mi top being a fraud now. Dis a fi wi script," SHE gets up from the table and dance and prance around the kitchen.

"You a real old time joker. A wha kinda scheme you ah gwan with now?" Desiree says.

SHE laughs. "For real, I'm going to set up my own ting and work with us, for us, in the community. I've had enough of this austerity language."

Desiree has heard SHE before and knows that she has good intentions, but good intentions can't change the world. Everything is falling apart now, the health service, the libraries, the local play-scheme and youth club have shut, and some of the tiny shops are struggling too.

Desiree opens up one of the carrier bags on the table. "SHE look at dis. I got this at Paradise Fashions," she says. SHE looks at the scarf but is distracted by her own thoughts. "They have got a sale on this week, someone told me they're struggling bad. We cut two joke about it and started to laugh, 'trouble in Paradise'..." Desiree tails off.

SHE sips her tea and composes herself, ready to tell her friend her big idea.

"Ok, I'm going to tell you exactly how we're going to run this," SHE says.

"We? When did the big we come into this?" says Desiree.

"Nuh mus we!" SHE replies, "ah weh u feel like. You must think I don't do my research."

"Hear dis karn ah go pop," Desiree replies.

"I am setting up a community interest company with a small loan of £5,000 to start. The university is running a scheme called 'Productive Margins'. I got a leaflet about it last time I was at Ubuntu." SHE says.

"You have time fi listen to Ubuntu, dem always get it wrong, trust me," Desiree replies.

"It's not Ubuntu runnin's. It's a scheme to encourage people to start community businesses. Me a go call it Life Chances. Weh u tink bout it?"

"Me love dat!" Desiree replies.

SHE jumps up out of the chair and demonstrates with her hands.

"We mek jewellery, we mek up, we meet up and talk da tings. The university sends along researchers to asks about our lives, as part of the deal, but dat alright, we have plenty to say. Although we haffi mine we self. What d'you think Desiree?" SHE says.

"Hey, you have great trust in dem my girl. How do u know dat dem na work fi da police?" Desiree says.

SHE busses up laughing. "Fi real, but sometimes we haffi tek chance."

"I thought the government had stopped all dem community business schemes?" Desiree asks.

"How you mean, it's EU money. Part of some international research project. I don't really know much about the scheme, but I do know they are offering start up grants to people like us," SHE says.

"That will take a lot of time. You have the time fi waste? And you will need somewhere to do it, won't you?" says Desiree.

"Look Desiree, I've been thinking about this for awhile. So if you're not on it let me know."

"And why you going on like that for?" Desiree replies.

SHE kisses her teeth, narrows her eyes and says, "Chu, huh. I'm going to rent one of the community enterprise units that the housing association is offering. They say they will give me the first six months free, suh dem sey, and we don't need to pay any rates. After that it's 'all in' we pay £200 a month and the only thing on top is electricity. So, you nuh sound like you interested, cos its pure negativity you're coming with."

"Backative you need," Desiree responds, "well, I've still got my chains at G4N, but when I have the time I will come and help you."

"Life Chances, is about taking charge, taking control. Wi nuh have time to sidown and wait on Babylon…" SHE rallies Desiree.

"Me and Shireen are going to a business planning workshop at Ubuntu and after four sessions our company will be ready," says SHE.

"Nu Shireen have trouble in her life. How she fi help you? I hear that her boy is having problems at school. He's being bullied and she won't have time to start a business. And she's been running up and down god knows where to help that pickney. And she got pull up to see the Head Teacher, just cos she told the bully to back off. How does that work, that Marlon gets all the trouble on him and his mother, when the other yoot is to blame?" says Desiree concerned.

"Everyone has something going on in their life it don't mean that she don't have something to share. She's smart, she's organized, has good ideas and as my bredrin I want to see her happy and feeling good about herself. How you mean, we haffi work and support each other. And the school ting, you know the answer to that. Melanin. One rule for us and another for them. Rass dem. And all Shireen did was go to the school gates to talk with the boy and now with their bright impertinence they call SS," says SHE .

"Nothing's changed," says Desiree.

"I'm going with her to sort it out with social services, I'm going to tell them that Marlon is not to blame and the other boy did it. And I'm going to tell them bout themself and get it dealt with. If they don't deal with it, I'm going to the MP and wi ah gu get serious," SHE is fully vexed now, speaking in the calm and measured voice she has when she's ready for action.

"This is the kind of thing I'm talking about with Life Chances. Yeah, we'll be sitting round making jewellery, and selling it for a profit. For sure. But it's also about all of us, all of us that get demonised by the government, violations and taking liberties with us. We need to come together to rewrite our story that has poisoned all of us, including them. They've destroyed every aspect of our lives, taken our names, language and have tried to take our dignity. Wi haffi tek it back. How can we change anything when they still continue to live lies and teach lies. Change the language, live UBUNTU, I say."

Desiree loves it when SHE gets in her flow. "Ah wat a way you hot. Ah trute you a talk bout."

She wasn't sure of how it would work, but Desiree knew SHE was onto something.... "Fiah inna Babylon."

Sitting on one of the famous, and it has to be said, rather uncomfortable, pink sofas on the orange floor at G4N, a curt email from Barry, cc'd to Jem, drops into Toby's inbox, basically repeating what he had already asked Toby to do and to do it asap. Obviously he wants to look the tough boss in front of Jem, thinks Toby, realising this will mean finding out exactly where all of the equipment is housed in the roll out of this 'agile' system. Toby closes his laptop and goes over to where Ady, Head of Operations, is playing Minecraft on his iPad.

"This Jem guy is putting the pressure on Barry for a double quick full audit of Deep Hole." Toby absent-mindedly kicks at the bean bag Ady is sitting on. "I don't want to trudge up and down the country looking at racked servers in forgotten basements."

Ady puts down his iPad and looks up at Toby.

"As you know Toby, during the opening procurement phase and scaling up, at least four main companies were brought in to build the systems architecture. They in turn subbed out a considerable amount of that work to their suppliers. What we have has been built on an agile approach, so at the outset we had no comprehension of final scale. I can tell you though that at least some of the stuff is in the Arctic area off Sweden, so I imagine you'll be keen on doing that visit in person," Ady tries smiling at his own joke, but loses confidence. A traditional geek, he's more comfortable online than in person, even with someone like Toby.

"Yeah, right, thanks Sheldon," says Toby. "Can you tell me where the most functional part of the roll out is?"

"Yep dude, it's in Bristol. But if you want to do a thorough audit you will need to go to more than just Bristol, Toby." replies Ady, plugging back into Minecraft.

"That's the way you'd do it, Ady. I ain't got time to piss around, bruv. I've got other fish to flambee, if you know what I mean." Toby taps the side of his nose and does his best gangsta swagger over to the Trojan coffee maker, that sits gleaming next to the vintage Hot Wheels race track.

Diane has set up a meeting with Barry Hamilton and asks around *The Image* office what people know about him. Not much comes back other than 'he's an Oxford man, popular with the current tribe, a fixer, ex-lobbyist, ex-CWL consultant, stints in Brussels and Strasbourg...'

The file on G4N on *The Image* intranet makes more interesting reading:

The Image – Intranet – 0980345G4N –
Formerly Great 4 Nations (in house nickname 'Great 4 No-one', not to be published) Chairman: Craig Tumbleton, nickname 'Fitter'.

Turnover: £8 billion (2015).
Services: Information and service design, government outsourced contracts, risk assessment services, cash handling and IT specialisation.
Employees: 230,000 Website: g4n.org.uk

Overview: G4N has been one of the most successful European multi-national companies in the area of outsourcing. Formed originally from the merger of two companies, Spendbröt AB (Sweden) and AnxIT (UK), the company now has global reach into government services, contracts and privatisation management in the UK, Sweden, mainland Europe and the USA.

Recently, the company has moved into large scale information technology and service design provision for countries moving towards triple 'S' products ('state streamlining services'). Has a consulting arm in the UK, specialising in failing or mis-managed technology programmes. Significant record of delivering management change and turnaround on budget.

Notes: G4N has employed several high profile candidates from UK and Swedish ministry offices or positions. Presently involved in the roll out of Universal Credit in the UK and Basic Income Guarantee (BIG) consulting for various European countries. Adoption of ideas by academic Ernst Negri that predicts the implementation of Basic Income Guarantees in Western States by 2040 as a result of the impact of artificial intelligence and automation. Negri chairs the influential 'Far Sight' programme at the Institute of the Future (part of UCL).

Negri, E, 2017. Why small became BIG. London: Clarity Sampson Atoll

Diane draws up a list of places to visit. She decides to go back to Bristol, then Northside Community Centre in Cardiff as she has good solid contacts in both places. Then up to the North West of England, covering some of the smaller towns like Bury, Bolton, Rochdale, St Helens and then over to Bradford. Nick has given her an expenses budget and a camera that looks beyond her basic knowledge of photography.

Diane decides to attend Isaiah's supervised visit herself, as she has taken on the case. She phones Sam half an hour before to make sure that everything is ok. She reassures Sam that if he and Rebecca can come to some agreement about child contact, which might include phasing in more frequent contact with Rebecca, she won't need to be involved anymore. At the moment there's a low risk of Rebecca being violent towards Sam and Debra is concerned how this might affect Isaiah.

The visit goes ahead in the park for one hour. Isaiah initially stays close to his dad, seemingly a bit shy of his mum. After a while he starts to warm up and Rebecca and Isaiah play together on the swings. Debra observes from a bench on one side of the play park. She mentally notes all of the child's behaviours and those of the parents. She is hoping that a staggered plan can be agreed, and Isaiah can resume his overnight stays at his mum's flat. Rebecca does need to undertake anger management sessions, and Debra sees that as a condition of moving forward.

Debra has noted down Rebecca's former drug use in the file, though she believes both Rebecca and Sam when they say she hasn't used since she was pregnant with Isaiah. Still you never know, once an addict, always an addict, she thinks. It's unusual for the child to live with the father when the family unit has broken down, but Sam seems capable and he has his mother involved in the childcare.

Sam places Isaiah on top of the slide and he slips down giggling. Rebecca picks him up at the bottom and gives him a hug. Debra smiles and nods at Rebecca, and the younger woman's smile sours into a scowl. Isaiah jumps down and runs towards the elephant on a spring and begins rapidly bouncing back and forth.

Debra observes the body language between the two parents. They are obviously uncomfortable with Debra there, but they play well with Isaiah and seemed to have agreed to focus on him rather than any issues they might have between them.

"I can't believe she just sits there and watches us like that, it's creepy," Rebecca says to Sam.

"Just pretend she's not there," says Sam. He knows Rebecca had a lot of bad experiences with Social Services when she was young. She winds him up, but he knows she has worked hard to turn her life around. He doesn't want to fight with her anymore, it's not good for Isaiah. He just wants to keep his head down and get through this and get back to normal.

The hour long visit comes to an end. Debra walks over and smiles at Isaiah. "Well that all went very well, didn't it?" she says to both parents.

"Yes, I think we should arrange another visit as soon as we can," says Sam.

Rebecca does not engage with Debra, her eyes are drawn down to a message on her phone. She begins tapping a reply.

"Can I go round mum's flat now?" asks Isaiah.

Toby and his two colleagues arrive at Bristol Temple Meads from London. They jump in a taxi to the Bristol Hotel, check in and head for the bar. The three men sit around and chat about work before moving on to a discussion about the potential of using linux boxes across the whole of Deep Hole. They know that the potential cost saving will be vast but the migration from typical IT purchasing will be a problem. Toby is not looking forward to detangling the messy layers of procurement and contractual obligations. He's brought Jeff with him who is the orange team's 'man of law'. Jeff cuts through procurement red tape 'like a knife through olive spread', according to Toby, who likes a joke with his team. Toby has learnt the all-important lesson that if you feel out of your depth then pull in some talent around you and move things on. With Deep Hole he feels more out of his depth than any other project he's worked on. But he is happy to busk it, because all the other people have fucked it up.

After three pints they decide to call it a day and head to their beds. Toby phones his girlfriend from his room and they end up arguing about their apartment in London Bridge. He's had enough of the life drawing classes she runs in the middle of their open plan loft space. They bring in hardly any money and cause major hassle as he has to de-rig his VR dome each week. Plus she's only been hiring old blokes as life models recently, and he has, quite frankly, had enough of being confronted by saggy old men's arses when he's on his way out to his Tai Chi class.

Chapter 3

April

Diane arrives at the head office of G4N near Embankment in London. Earlier in the day she had a meeting with Nick at *The Image* and he suggested she tell them that she is interested in the role the private sector can play in solving the often complex delivery of government legislation, such as the new Universal Credit system. That way G4N looks good and maybe they can show some balance between the conflicting experiences of Universal Credit clients in the roll out testing areas such as Bristol, one of the stops on her tour of Britain. Diane respects Nick's experience and is happy to go with his suggestions.

Diane announces herself at the desk and signs the register. She is given a badge and asked to wait for the press officer to arrive. She waits for half an hour and no-one appears. She asks again at the desk and is told that it's a busy day because the end of year work is happening across all departments. Diane is pretty sure she is being made to wait on purpose, an opening power play to let her know who's in charge. Pathetic really. She sighs and opens up her laptop and starts going through her emails. Fifty minutes late, the press officer finally arrives and greets her.

"Hi, I'm Victoria, I'm the press officer here, I'll take you up to meet Barry. I hope you haven't been waiting long. We'll also have our external PR people in the room for the interview, ok?" She smiles hard showing a row of perfect white teeth. Her "ok" is more of a statement than a question.

"Yes, that's fine. Will I be able to record the interview with him?"

"Yes, all fine, we may ask you to avoid certain questions but we will tell you that during the interview and we trust that you will be understanding on those elements?"

"Of course," says Diane. She now feels slightly nervous but is enjoying being on the inside of the company she's heard so much about. They get in the elevator together and Victoria presses button 15. The lift doors seem to take ages to close. Diane and Victoria stand side by side, facing forward, neither of them speaking. Finally the doors close and the lift glides up to the requested floor.

"Can I get you anything, Diane? We have Pomegranate and Moss San Pellegrino, or Zero Max Zero Pepsi. Or perhaps an Oolong First Flush?" Victoria asks. Diane has no idea what the last choice was, sounds like a brand of toilet cleaner. "No, I'm fine, thanks."

Victoria escorts her over to Barry's office. She is introduced to two people.

"This is Julia and James. They are both from Friends PR our external support on special projects," Victoria says.

Diane shakes their hands and notices James's Giuseppe Zanetti sneakers. Julia is wearing a Caroline Charles 'Mikado' dress. Diane recognises it from a feature *The Image* did on her latest collection last month. They both exude the kind of quiet self-confidence that comes with a private education and a six-figure salary.

"Diane, it's great to meet you. I read your piece on misogyny and transphobia, it was fabulous, very insightful." Julia smiles at Diane, maintaining steady eye contact.

Diane is flattered and, much to her annoyance, blushes.

"Thanks," she replies briefly, trying to control the heat rising up her cheeks.

Diane makes a move towards the chair at the head of the table, but is cut off by Julia nimbly pulling out a chair at the side and offering it to Diane. Julia glides smoothly to the head of the table and sits down, motioning to James to sit on her right. Victoria is left standing by the door.

"Victoria, darling. Would you mind taking notes? I left my Birkin at the Groucho last night and it had absolutely everything in it." Julia smiles intensely at Diane as she speaks, as if Diane knows exactly what was in Julia's bag.

Diane glances over at Victoria who doesn't look at all happy with the request.

"I'll buzz Stephen, my PA, and he can come and take notes," Victoria replies icily.

Julia nods her approval. "So, Diane. What will be the main focus of your article for us?"

The 'for us' irritates Diane enough to get her back on track.

"Well, Julia, we're interested in the impact of Universal Credit on real people, and whether the Government rhetoric around 'making work pay' is actually working on the ground. And of course how Universal Credit is implemented by G4N. It will be a series of articles loosely based on my retreading the route taken by Ivan Dunhouse-Jones in 2009 around deprived areas of the country."

"And how is it going so far?" James asks.

Diane can see that this is a set-up pre-interview before the main man appears. It feels a bit tiresome, but she decides to play along.

"We know that there have been problems with the procurement but we also know that overall the system has good intentions. Nobody thinks that keeping people on benefits for the rest of their lives is a good idea. So, we partly want to show how UC can give people a chance of a working life. That's it really," Diane replies.

James and Julia appear to be happy with the answers and nod at Victoria.

"Ok, I'll see if Barry's finished his meeting with the CFO. Shouldn't be too long now..." Victoria says and walks out of the office. James and Julia comment on the view of the Thames from the office. Diane gets her digital recorder out of her bag and places it on the table.

Barry waltzes into the office and greets James and Julia. He turns to Diane, shaking her firmly by the hand.

"Hello, you must be Diane... *The Image*... if we can get something positive in your rag we'll be very happy. You will be nice about me won't you?"

Diane has been told about Barry's charm and hubris.

"Julia that is a fabulous dress, M&S?" Barry quips.

"No, it's Caroline Charles..."

Victoria hides a smirk by turning to Diane. "Is it on?" she asks, gesturing towards the voice recorder.

"Yes," Diane replies.

"Well you'll get the same from me, regardless of whether it's being recorded or not," says Barry. He has been told earlier by Julia to keep moving around the room and to keep it light. Avoid any questions about applicant procedure, talk about digital by design and the value it gives back to the government and the clients. Keep talking about the core aims. Get people back into work, make work pay, design a system that makes this easy. Any awkward questions about poverty then wait for Julia to give him a steer.

"Ok, Diane, all yours..." Victoria gestures.

"Can you tell me about the revision in the procurement procedures for Universal Credit and what we now know as Deep Hole," asks Diane.

"Sorry, Diane, sorry Barry to interrupt," says Julia. "We're not going to refer to the IT system as Deep Hole, we're going to talk about systems service design, sorry about that..."

"Ok, can you tell me about how the systems service design will be developed by G4N, now that you have the head contract? What are your plans over the next few months?" Diane asks.

"Sorry, Diane, sorry everyone. Can we ask that question slightly differently? Can we discuss Universal Credit more broadly as G4N has only just acquired the lead on this one..."

"Hang on, Julia, I think that's a good question, don't you Diane?" says Barry. Earlier the agreement was to unhinge Diane with some interruptions regardless of the question with a tilt to Barry to play 'good cop'.

Diane has experienced this kind of PR tactic before – opaque transparency with a huge dollop of spin.

"Well, Diane, the systems service design we are looking at will be digital by design, it will be simple to use, it will give people straightforward questions and overall it will assist people back into work, because they will be able to see that work pays. That's what IDJ wants, we are simply the servants here," Barry finally answers, emanating confidence in his bespoke suit and made-to-measure shoes. Julia lets that one run, although she notes down an overuse of 'simple' in Barry's approach. Victoria switches her phone to silent and begins plugging some texts into it.

"What have you found out so far in the early roll out of the scheme?"

Diane asks.

"We have found out that the system needs to upscale to take on board many different circumstances and being digital by design means that we can do that. However, prior to our involvement this hadn't been thought through enough. So we have people on the ground, right now in fact, working on ways to make the system design more sensitive. Because a core factor is that work needs to be seen to pay..."

The interview lasts for around 45 minutes with Diane not getting much more than stock phrases about 'systems service design' and 'work in progress'. She feels frustrated that there is no obvious information about how real people experience the process.

"Can you tell me what your data shows at the moment about successful applicants? Do they in fact prefer this system to the old benefits system? How will claimants deal with monthly, rather than fortnightly payments, with having payments made electronically into their bank accounts?" Diane asks.

Julia interjects like lightning. "That question is best answered not by us but by the Department for Work and Pensions, sorry about that..." she says.

"I can give you my opinion," Barry says. "Some people will not be able to manage their money well enough and they will need help. This is all part of getting off long term benefits isn't it? It's the ability to take on your own affairs and not be nannied along, nobody wants that do they? That's what we had under the previous lot, a growing disconnect between the working world and signing on," Barry answers.

Julia jumps in.

"That is Barry's own opinion of course – not the official line of G4N. Barry has his views but G4N is all about streamlining services for the public. Sorry about that, that's right isn't it, Barry?" Julia says firmly.

"Yes, that's right, that's my opinion," says Barry.

"I am interested in your opinion, Barry, go on?" says Diane.

"Barry has now given you the allocated time for the interview," Julia interjects, "as I'm sure you'll understand, Barry is a busy man. Diane, thank you for coming,"

Diane reaches over and shuts off the recorder. She leaves the office with air kisses from Julia and a double handed handshake from James. As friendly as vipers, Diane thinks. Victoria escorts her to the reception desk and takes her security badge.

"Really looking forward to your piece, when will it be out, do let us know?"

Back upstairs Julia carries out a debrief with Barry.

"You're going to have to do quite a few of these and not always with people on-side. The movement around the office was good and generally the answers were fine about service design but remember to keep away from talking about people and users, oh, and you're over using the word simple, try something like 'one click' or 'effortless'."

"Thank you Julia. I will dig out my thesaurus over the weekend, or perhaps there is an app I can download to my phone? Expand my obviously narrow vocabulary while riding the tube to work in the morning?" Whilst Barry was fine with Julia adopting a pedagogical tone with the lefty hackette from the worthier-than-thou *Image*, he wasn't going to put up with it himself.

Flustered, Julia lets out a nervous giggle, quite at odds with the cool image she projects.

"Gosh sorry Barry, I didn't mean to infer that you.."

Barry holds up a hand. "Let's leave it there shall we." He nods a dismissal and walks off to see the CFO again. It's going be a long day.

Toby has been in Bristol with his two colleagues for over a week. They haven't made much progress, having spent most of the time going through paperwork and examining working procedures.

"We could do most of this back in London, if they'd put it all on the shared server or re-patched a VPN into their server. Why are we here looking at things locally?" Toby questions.

His two colleagues have no idea but they do know that audit means 'audit', checking everything over and creating an asset list. At least the asset list is mostly done.

It's day eight of their Bristol jaunt and they decide to arrive early at G4N offices and take a look at the server racks. At 7.30am none of the senior management team are in. There is some confusion about the 'AAA' passes that were supposed to have been sorted at the beginning of the week. After some phone calls at the front desk, the passes are located and handed out.

Toby and his colleagues are taken into the server room, failing to acknowledge Desiree, whom they pass in the corridor. They walk over to Derek, the 'sysops' guy, and question him on the current performance of 'Agile Plus', the upgraded software for processing claims for Universal Credit.

Derek tells it like it is. "To be honest guys, it's pretty ratty, we've got 30,000 emulation cases pulled over from the farm database with real data parsing into it. But the performance is well below expectation. We still need to partition things off to reduce query time and the problem will be, that as the case load piles up in the real world this will fall over big style."

"Ok Derek, so what do you suggest we do?" asks Toby.

"Another full rewrite of the SQL, chaps," says Derek, "and some time spent on scaling the systems architecture..." Desiree walks past them and is finally noticed.

"What's she doing in here?" asks Toby.

"She's a Triple A cleaner," replies Derek.

"Well tell her to go and clean somewhere else, Derek, and not in here. This is a secure area, not just anyone can come in here..."

"Like I said, she has Access All Areas. Desiree is absolutely rock solid and signed off to clean for the Queen if necessary."

"Well, Derek, cleaning is not required in this area for the next six weeks, so please advise the cleaner accordingly," counters Toby.

Desiree stops and turns round. She knows who Toby is, she's heard Derek talking to the other IT workers about some big shot computer whizz coming down from London to look at Deep Hole. She can't believe the pasty-faced streak of piss standing in front of her in his black hoody and sad boy sneakers could possibly know anything worth knowing.

"I am a real person you know, you can speak to me," Desiree answers. She can see Derek is annoyed with Toby, but she doesn't need him fighting her fights.

Toby replies sweetly, "I'm sorry love, that was out of order of me, we've had a pretty unsuccessful visit so far…many apologies…not a good week to catch me…My name's Toby, how about getting us a brew, eh?" Toby proffers.

Fuckin' cheek, thinks Desiree, slowly looking him up and down. She had been thinking about telling this Toby about the strange sounds Deep Hole had been making, but now she decides not to because he's too *bloody facety*.

"I ain't your servant. You don't know who I am. Don't you be talking to me like that you jumped up little twerp. Get your own dyam tea and get yourself some manners at the same time." Desiree sucks her teeth, turns her back on Toby and walks towards the exit.

Derek stifles a laugh as Toby watches Desiree leave, the blush on his cheeks making him look like a *dyam fool.*

"Zan where?" asks Debra, dunking a Hobnob in her tea.

"Zantonica. It's an archipelago of four islands off the coast of Somalia. A little known paradise in the Arabian Sea," Will reads from his computer screen. "Look at those beaches."

Debra puts her mug down on Will's desk and cranes her neck round his computer. Images of golden sands, gentle palm trees and hazy blue seas fill the screen.

Debra sits back down with a sigh. "I can't remember the last time I went on holiday." She crunches the rest of the Hobnob, spraying crumbs as she speaks.

"Why would someone from Zan, Zan.."

"Zantonica," Will interjects, taking a handkerchief from his pocket and wiping the crumbs from his desk.

"Sorry. I haven't eaten since breakfast, I've had one visit after another. My last visit ran over time and then my car wouldn't start. I had to ask the client to give me a push down the hill!" Debra laughs, and starts rummaging in her bag for her case files.

Will folds his hands in front of him and rests them on his desk giving Debra his best managerial frown.

"Perhaps I can suggest some time management training Debra?" Will was on secondment from Haringey Social Services, covering Marie's maternity leave. He was a lot younger than Debra and seemed to feel the need to assert his authority on a regular basis. Marie was a bit grumpy but at least she had experience, she'd been in social work for 20 years and Debra felt she could always rely on her support. The job was hard enough without someone young enough to be her son patronising her.

Debra smiles her reply. She has found it best to politely ignore Will's suggestions.

Will looks back at his computer. "Her name is Secnach E'fil and she's a PhD student doing comparative research on the welfare systems of the UK and Zantonica. She's been based at Haringey Social Services for the past couple of weeks. Something I set up actually. A favour for my old alma mater, the University of London. And I thought a sojourn to Bristol would be interesting for her."

No need to look quite so proud of yourself, thinks Debra, it's not exactly a radical idea.

"So as our longest serving social worker," Will smiles, his tone of voice making 'longest serving' sound like a euphemism for 'oldest', "I'd like you to take Secnach on some of your visits over the next few weeks."

"Yes that's fine," Debra replies. More work is exactly what I need, she thinks to herself.

"So let's get down to business. What upcoming visits do you have that Secnach can accompany you on? Let's start with Marlon Oates shall we? I see the school have been in contact?" queries Will.

Debra puts on her glasses and opens up Marlon's file.

"Yes. They've informed us that Marlon was in a fight last week. They know the family has been involved with social services in the past and the head is also concerned about the behaviour of some of his African-

Caribbean pupils. The school has told us that a woman called SHE has shared parental responsibility with Shireen, the boy's biological mother. So I've made an appointment to visit SHE and Shireen at the family home on Thursday. It's an unusual set up for a family from that cultural background and I wonder if that's contributing to Marlon's disruptive behaviour?"

"Hmm yes, it could be," Will replies as he starts to look through the large pile of files Debra has placed on his desk. "With no disrespect to the family, that's not an overly interesting case for Secnach is it?...what else do you have coming up? Let's have a look. Ah, here, what about this, I seem to remember this one is a bit more, erm, complex?" Will holds up Isaiah Bailey's file.

Will's tone makes Debra feel uncomfortable. Thank god Marie is back in eight months, thinks Debra.

"I'm also due to visit them on Thursday. A neighbour of Isaiah's mother informed us that Rebecca Gordon had left her seven year old son on his own for approximately four hours in the early evening. The neighbour said that this is not the first time it has happened, but we only have his word for that. Isaiah is not resident with Rebecca, but lives with his father, Sam Bailey. Sam and Rebecca split up when Isaiah was three. Rebecca is already known to us. She comes from quite a chaotic family background and was in and out of care when she was a child. She has a history of substance abuse but has been clean since she was pregnant with Isaiah." Debra replies.

"So she's had some sort of relapse then? Back on drugs?" Will asks.

"She says she was called into work on short notice and had no alternative but to leave Isaiah on his own, as she didn't want to lose her job. Sam and Rebecca don't get on too well, which is why she didn't ask him to look after Isaiah. I think she wants to prove to everyone she can manage. Sam has quite an overbearing mother." Debra explains. "I've arranged a series of supervised visits with Sam, Rebecca and Isaiah. The first one went well."

"Great. I'm sure that will be a very interesting case for Secnach. A long term client with a dysfunctional background, in and out of care, a single parent with a young child and a drug problem. Now I'm very sorry but I've got a 4pm Skype. I'll email you Secnach's contact details and perhaps you can arrange a meeting time and place with her?"

Will looks at Debra in a way that indicates their meeting is over.

Debra starts to replace the files in her bag. "Rebecca doesn't have a drug problem any more and she's not a single parent. She co-parents Isaiah with Sam," she insists.

"Yes, yes," replies Will, as he looks at his computer screen and starts to log into Skype, "Let me know how it goes with Secnach."

Feeling like she's just been dismissed by some self-important teenager, Debra takes her mug from Will's desk, puts her bag over her shoulder and goes out into the open plan office.

At her desk she googles 'cheap flights to Zantonica' and checks her diary for the next day.

"Get up, stand up, stand up for..." A hand reaches out to shut off the music alarm. SHE stretches over to kiss and love up with her husband of five years. Clyde returns the kiss and intimate snuggle with his wife.

"Tea or hot chocolate, my King?" asks SHE, leisurely rolling over.

"Lemon and hot water please, thank you," Clyde replies.

SHE sits up and reaches for her dressing gown, it is cold this morning, *rahtid*. She makes her way to the bathroom, washes her face and brushes her teeth. Her back is still aching from piggybacking the children yesterday. She laughs and muses to herself, I must stop acting like I'm fifteen. After going to the toilet and thoroughly washing her hands with the luxurious Avocado and Honey wash (*'mmmm'*), she quietly closes the bathroom door.

As SHE walks to the children's bedrooms, the heating turns itself on, and she wraps her gown tightly round her body.

SHE opens the first bedroom door. "Morning, time to get up." She kisses her child on the cheek and strokes his face. Groans and moans can be heard and an almost audible "morning mum" from her son.

"I'm going to wake up your sister, then bathe and go and wake Shireen dem alright?"

"Alright mum," Syka answers between yawns.

Before leaving SHE draws the curtains, to the vexation of her son. She smiles and leaves as Syka throws the quilt back over himself.

Next to awaken is her daughter Malaya. As SHE opens the door the light hits her eyes forcing her to pull back and frown. As she enters the room her daughter greets her with a smile.

"Morning mum. I've been awake a long time. I've just finished my book." SHE strokes her face and kisses her child.

"Morning to you too. Was it a good book?" she asks.

"Yes it was sick. I'm going to read it again."

"That's fine but not before you bathe and have breakfast, ok?" SHE tells her, smiling softly. Malaya gets up, hugs her mum and begins to organise her school bag. SHE leaves to get herself bathed and dressed, calling behind her, "I am going over the road, one of you make lemon and water for your daddy."

Once dressed and bathed, creamed and hair tackled, SHE unlocks the front door, slips across the traffic free road and uses her key to open Shireen's front door. The house is in darkness and music can be heard coming from one of the bedrooms.

SHE climbs up the stairs quickly and knocks on everyone's doors. The last door is Shireen's. Knock, knock. SHE slowly opens the door and puts her head round.

"You want breakfast this morning, Shir?"

From under the cover Shireen answers. "Morning mi fren, how woulda manage without you? Yes please, whatevers runnin."

SHE laughs, still at the doorway. "What would we do without each other, sis. I am going to wake everyone, come when you are ready. And remember that social worker is coming over in a bit and we're going to set things straight about Marlon and that school bully."

Shireen throws back the cover and looks at her friend. "That is too much drama, too early."

"Don't worry, I'll be there to support you, like I promised."

Shireen smiles and yawns. “See you in a bit,” They both respond together.

SHE then knocks on all the children's doors again, this time entering and waking them all up. Everyone is tired, but they all greet her with a good morning kiss. SHE returns their kisses with the added stroke of their face, the same wake up routine as dem born.

“Brush your teeth and bathe before you come for breakfast please, all of you,” she says sternly. Marlon rolls his eyes. SHE notices. “Especially you Marlon, nobody want to see sweetcorn teet and tinkin body, mi boy.” They all laugh, and the morning hustle and bustle begins.

SHE goes downstairs, turns on lights and draws the curtains. SHE shouts, “See you in a bit, breakfast soon ready.” She closes the door and returns home to the smell of toast, spiced tea and the sound of the local radio station.

The thing that strikes Secnach the most, after two months in the UK, is not the weather, though that has been pretty bad. And it was not the food, which again, has been pretty hit and miss. It is the general sense of despondency she’s encountered. The professionals she’s met work hard and care about their jobs, but everyone seems so over-stretched and tangled up in systems.

She finishes checking her emails at what is becoming her favourite cafe. The coffee is strong and served in sky blue bowls with golden rims that remind her of home. Plus they make the most delicious carrot cake, an English delicacy they serve in astonishingly large slices. She goes out onto the street to where she has agreed to meet Debra, a social worker Will has arranged for her to shadow over the coming weeks.

A car pulls up alongside her and a harassed looking woman with glasses winds down the window. “Seeknatch?” “Yes, but it is pronounced Secnach,” Secnach answers with a smile.

“Oh yes, sorry, I’m no good with names. My brain is a bit frazzled. Been doing staff training and paperwork all day. Jump in. Our first visit is just round the corner,” Debra replies.

Debra moves her bag of files from the passenger seat and Secnach gets in.

"So, Zantonica? Quite different from the UK, I imagine? Better weather for one thing I'm sure." Debra switches on the windscreen wipers as the light drizzle turns into a downpour.

"Yes that is true. But the rain makes for a 'green and pleasant land' does it not?"

Debra laughs, "I think it's more dark satanic mills round here."

Debra turns the corner and pulls the car up outside a row of terraced houses. Secnach looks at the row of two-up, two-down's. People have no space in this country, all squashed together living on top of each others lives. Secnach has seen a lot of generosity in the places she has visited in Bristol and London, generosity borne from adversity. She still cannot believe that a first-world country has a growing rate of child poverty. In her country, this would simply not be tolerated.

"So our first visit is a non-traditional family unit, if you know what I mean. The biological mother is called Shireen, and the other woman, SHE, has shared parental responsibility for Shireen's children, including Marlon who we've come to discuss today. The school contacted us as Marlon was in a fight a week ago and the head has been having trouble with his African-Caribbean pupils, the boys in particular."

"So we are here because Marlon is African-Caribbean and has been in a fight?" asks Secnach, puzzled.

"Well that's not quite the way I would put it," Debra replies. "The school has concerns and we are following up on those concerns. The family is already known to social services. Let's go shall we. I have a lot of visits to get through today. I'll introduce you and if you can observe without talking, that would be appreciated."

"Yes of course, I am here to observe only," Secnach replies.

"Right, I have an umbrella somewhere." Debra rifles around on the backseat and pulls out a mangled umbrella from under the pile of shopping.

Debra checks her ID is visible as they wait for the door to be answered.

"Hi Shireen?" Asks Debra. The woman nods. "I'm Debra from Social Services, and this is Seeknatch. May we come in?"

"Of course, come right in and sit down. Would you like a coffee?" Shireen asks.

"That is most kind of you, but I have just had one," replies Secnach.

"So, Marlon is at school?" asks Debra.

SHE comes into the room. "Yes of course he is. You know we'll need to finish up in half an hour as Shireen needs to go pick him up."

"Great, you must be SHE? I'm Debra and this is Seeknatch. Seeknatch is a PhD student from Zantonica who's researching the UK's welfare system. She's come along this afternoon to observe our meeting. Is that ok?"

"No it's not ok actually. No-one told Shireen that – what's your name?" SHE looks at Secnach.

"Secnach."

"No-one told Shireen that Secnach would be coming along to the meeting."

"I'm so sorry," Secnach starts to get up from her chair, "I did not mean to offend you. I shall leave."

SHE smiles and clasps her hand. "No need to apologise, my sister, it is not your fault. You should not have been put in this position."

Secnach smiles. Her first impulse is to try and diffuse the tension in the room, but does not want to over-step the mark with Debra. She is here to observe after all, and she is interested to see how Debra will handle the situation.

Shireen goes into the kitchen, returns with a plate of biscuits and puts them on the table. "Marlon made them yesterday, he loves cooking."

Debra gets a file out of her bag and starts to read.

"So Mr Overton the headmaster phoned us a couple of weeks ago..." Debra starts.

"Hang on," Shireen takes her phone out of her pocket, presses record and puts the phone on the table. "I'm sorry but you can't really do that...” Debra reaches over for the phone.

“Yes she can,” replies SHE.

“This is a confidential meeting about a child’s welfare so I’m afraid due to data protection, I must ask you...” SHE interrupts Debra. “Shireen can record this meeting, it’s within her legal rights.”

“This is true,” Secnach agrees, “I was reading about this subject in preparation for this meeting. A parent can record a social work meeting if it is for their personal use.”

“Yes, well, thank you Seeknatch. I was about to say, before the interruption, that if you are recording the meeting, I must ask you to keep the recording for your personal use only. No sharing on Facebook or whatever,” Debra frowns at Secnach and reaches for a biscuit.

“Why would you think Shireen would post personal information about Marlon and her family on social media for all the world to see?” SHE narrows her eyes and shakes her head at Debra.

Debra takes off her glasses and smiles. “Yes. Sorry. I meant no offence. Shall we start again?“

“I suggest we do,“ says SHE.

“Have a seat, please,” Debra gestures towards the sofa.

“Thank you for offering me a seat in my own yard,” SHE sits down on the edge of the sofa.

Secnach catches SHE murmuring, this woman is a real eediat. Secnach looks over at Debra and can see by the tightness of her lips that she heard it too.

“So Shireen, you’re the biological mother of Marlon, is that right?” asks Debra.

“Er, yeah,” Shireen replies, looking puzzled.

“And Marlon resides at both of your houses?” Debra asks SHE.

“Marlon resides with his mum. He stays with me from time to time,” SHE answers.

"So there is no set pattern to his visits with you?"

"Why would there be a set pattern? He stays once in a while, all the children do."

Debra starts to write in the file. Shireen and SHE share a look, Shireen shrugs and frowns at SHE, slightly shaking her head. Secnach is interested in how much information is being shared in this situation non-verbally. She doesn't think that Debra is picking up on all that is going on. Again she feels like she would like to intervene. She can tell that Debra is working from her file rather than from what's happening in the room.

"Perhaps the uncertainty of the situation is unsettling Marlon? If he's not sure when he's going to see his other mum, and is confused about his parenting...may be this is why he's acting out at school?"

SHE is really pissed off now. "Are you for real, what other mum are you talking about?"

Debra looks down at her notes. "The school told us you have shared parental responsibility for Marlon with Shireen. I'm assuming as you live in separate houses you're no longer together?" Debra gives a saccharine smile.

SHE laughs. This woman seems to have everything back to front. Why must she always have to fight so hard to get these people to actually hear what she is saying. "We don't have shared parental responsibility, I don't know why the school told you that. Shireen and I have been best friends since school. We look out for each other, and each other's children. Are there any other questions you wanna ask?"

"Oh right, sorry. I'll just amend my notes," Debra, flustered, takes a pen out of her bag.

"I'm afraid I'll have to ask you to leave then, SHE." Debra says, looking up from the file. "As I said before, this meeting is confidential and about a child whom I now know is not your legal responsibility."

SHE is thinking this was what Debra was trying to get at all along. Dyam wrenk. SHE folds her arms and positions herself on the edge of the sofa.

Debra turns and smiles at Shireen "And forgive me for that

misunderstanding, I was just going by what the school told me."

"I would like SHE to stay," replies Shireen.

"Well, I'm sorry but there really is no need for her to be here..."

"Look Debra." replies SHE, "you've come here, and no offence to Secnach, bringing someone with you that Shireen wasn't told was coming, and putting them in an uncomfortable position, where you expected her to accept your decision. Shireen decides who comes to her yard, not you. And now you're asking me to leave. You are passing your place. Shireen wants me here to support her. She wants me here to witness this meeting, which to tell you the truth, after this conversation, is turning out to be a dyam good idea. Plus, as Secnach can tell you, a parent is perfectly within their rights to have whom they choose to support them."

Secnach looks at SHE but says nothing. She can see that SHE is looking after her friend and admires the way she is taking charge of the situation. Secnach also feels for Debra who has been given the wrong information on which to base the interview.

"And I don't understand why this visit is taking place anyway. Marlon has one fight at school, which by the way was started by another boy, an older, much bigger white boy, and all of a sudden Shireen has the social called on her. Have you gone to visit the white boy's parents? Nah I don't know why I even bothered to ask that. And Shireen gets called into the school but do the white boy's parents? No. No they don't. Shireen gets treated like some sort of criminal just because she told the boy not to pick on her son. Shireen could have told Marlon on a number of occasions to just lick him down straight. She did not. Shireen and Marlon have followed the school's procedures and now he has been physically attacked – again – for the how muchintime. So now Marlon has defended himself. Does he not have the right to do that? The head teacher had the audacity to call security!" SHE kisses her teeth.

SHE is calm. She speaks slowly and deliberately. She's not going let this woman get away with bullying and intimidating Shireen. She is not bothered if Debra thinks that she is another angry black woman. Kiss her teeth. SHE is angry, but she knows Shireen is worried. Her family has a history with the social services and that kind of baggage is hard to get rid of. So SHE is calm.

Debra is tired. She is tired of going into situations with the wrong information. She is tired of always being seen as the 'bad guy'. She is tired of being overworked and unappreciated. She is tired of social workers being portrayed in the media as child snatching busybodies. But mostly she is just tired. Debra puts her half eaten cookie back on the plate. "I'm sorry, we've got off on the wrong foot. I'm here to talk to Shireen about what happened, to get her viewpoint. I understand a parent's wish to protect her child. We're acting on the information the school passed on to us, which I can see now contains some inaccuracies. Shireen perhaps you could tell me what happened?"

"Ok," says Shireen, "I know you've come here to do your job, but as you've just pointed out you started on the wrong foot, and I have no control over that, just as I have no control over preventing my son being bullied, or making sure the school protects my children whilst in their care."

Debra sits down and Shireen tells her about Marlon and how he's being bullied at school and how that makes her feel and how the school has been doing nothing about it, and that she's frustrated and vexed.

"Oh, so I can see now that there is really no reason for us to be here," Debra says.

"No there isn't, you need to get up to the school and ask the parents of the child who's been bullying my son if they know what their child's doing, and ask the school what have they done and what are they doing?" Shireen insists.

Debra makes copious notes. She will speak to the school and ask them to be much more clear about referrals in the future. This seems like an obvious case of racial discrimination to her. And it's wasting her time.

"I'm sorry, I will speak to the Head at St Lawrence's and make sure they give you an apology," Debra replies. "That's the least they can do," says SHE.

Debra and Secnach leave the house and head off for the next visit with Sam, Rebecca and Isaiah.

"Right, I better just make a quick call to Sam to check it's ok for you to come along to the supervised visit. If you want to get in I'll just be a minute," Debra says to Secnach as she unlocks the car.

Secnach gets in the car and fastens her seatbelt. Debra sees her watching through the windscreen as she talks briefly on her mobile. At least Debra is providing Secnach with some full-on real life situations. She wonders what Secnach thinks of it all. It's hard to tell with the polite and inscrutable demeanour she projects.

"All ok?" Secnach asks.

"Yep, let's go. The park we're meeting in is about a ten minute drive. I'll fill you in on the case as I drive," Debra replies as she starts the engine.

The sun has come out by the time they arrive. They pull into the car park and make their way to the playground. Sam and Isaiah arrive next, followed almost immediately by Rebecca.

Debra does the introductions and then she and Secnach retire to one of the multi-coloured benches that line the playground.

Rebecca feels more at ease this time, and she and Isaiah sit for a while on the swings, gently swinging back and forth and chatting about his day at school. She misses him so much. They start playing tag and Sam joins in, chasing after Isaiah and then swerving to tag Rebecca. Sam and Rebecca have been chatting on the phone quite a bit and getting on much better. He seems to be making a real effort to keep Rebecca in the loop about Isaiah and she really appreciates it. Sometimes she can hear his mother muttering in the background, but chooses to ignore it. That woman never thought she was good enough for her boy. Well she'll show her. Isaiah was her son and there was nothing that could change that.

Towards the end of the allocated hour, Debra goes over to chat to them. Rebecca stiffens slightly. She doesn't want the hour to be over and she certainly doesn't want to be talking to Debra again.

"Hi Isaiah, would you like to go and have a chat with Secnach whilst I talk to your parents. I know she's interested in what kind of things kids in the UK like to do after school and may be you could tell her what games you like to play?" asks Debra.

Isaiah feels uncertain and looks at his dad for guidance.

"Yep, off you go Isaiah. I'm sure Secnach would love to know about your X-men comics, we'll just be a minute." Sam squeezes Isaiah's shoulder and turns back to Debra.

"So we've been talking, on the phone of course, and Rebecca and I would like to move things along and get back to normal. How about an end to the supervised visits, I know Isaiah finds them weird. Rebecca could come round my flat a couple of times a week and I would be there with Isaiah the whole time," Sam suggests.

Rebecca did not like the idea that Sam will be supervising her with her own son, but has agreed to go along with it for Isaiah's sake. Just as long as Sam's mum isn't there.

"Well I'm not sure about that Sam, Rebecca. I think that might be moving too fast. I need to see the reports from Rebecca's anger management class before we can move forward. I have asked her tutor for the report and I'm give him a ring after our meeting to hurry it along," Debra replies.

"I don't see what anger management has to do with the one mistake I made, which was to leave Isaiah on his own, safe in my flat, for four hours. Once. I don't shout at Isaiah, I don't smack him. How can the anger management classes that you've made me go to have anything to do with me being a mum to my son?" Rebecca's voice gets louder as she becomes more frustrated.

"Now Rebecca, just calm down. We're just trying to do what's best for Isaiah."

Rebecca knows she has to go now, or she will lose it with this woman. She marches out of the playground, slamming the gate behind her. She hates the fact that Debra's judgement of her as someone with 'anger problems' makes her angry, and so fulfils Debra's opinion of her. But who wouldn't get angry in this situation?

"I'll be in touch tomorrow," Debra says to Sam as they both watch Rebecca walk out of the park.

Sam is disappointed. Rebecca had been doing so well. All she needed to do was hang in there for a bit longer, go through the routine and then they would be left alone to raise their son together. The more she pushed, the more they pushed back.

"Look she's trying her best you know," Sam says. "She's not an angry person, she's just finding it hard that people are judging her on her past."

Isaiah tugs on Sam's coat sleeve. "Come on dad, let's go home."

Diane spends a week back in London, writing, arranging visits and ringing up contacts. She decides to go back to Bristol, then Cardiff and then head up north. Before leaving she speaks to Nick on the phone.

"I've got the first bit ready for you, I'll send it over now..." she says.

The Faceless Society – Digital by Design

Following in the great man's footsteps, I have begun my journey around Ivan Dunhouse-Jones's Universal Credit project. His form of 'Compassionate Conservatism' is digital by design. After all, everyone is online nowadays, aren't they? We're all 'agile', streamlined by technology. No need for a human interface now, in the disappearing welfare state.

So, here it goes, with apologies to Gil Scott Heron:

The Faceless Society will be digital by design, there will be no need for pen nor paper, for the man or woman across a desk. The Faceless Society will revolutionise. Everything will change and everything will stay the same. The Faceless Society will be digital by design. There will be no need to speak to anyone, and no-one will speak to you. And it will be syndicated to every channel. It will be on every screen, every device, every medium. The Faceless Society is digital by design. The Faceless Society will keep your family together, regardless of the weather. It will steer you down the right road, the path where work always pays and everyone gets straight As. The Faceless Society. Digital by Design.

The project is a vast overhaul of public welfare and recasting of thirty years of unwieldy benefits that stand as a reminder that in Britain we like filling in forms, and lots of them. At first sight Universal Credit, or 'UC', as it will be commonly known, streamlines six existing benefits into one online form with the overall objective of simplification and making work pay. This of course means saving costs and making it clear to the claimant what they can get each month. And there lies a critical point; it will come to the claimant via a single monthly payment direct into their bank account. The architecture to make this wonder happen, however, has not been without problems. Dismantling the gargantuan mass of red tape associated with all the previous benefits and drawing up a system that works at source for everyone has been a vast undertaking. More than anyone imagined, in fact, to the point where the cost over-runs have been in the billions.

Again, I tried to get hold of Ivan Dunhouse-Jones, Secretary of State for Work and Pensions, but to no avail. He has been under huge pressure in the last six months to get Universal Credit up to scratch, following a series of revelations about the failure of the first 'agile' version of the system. 'Agile' is the slightly buzzy, but slightly past its sell by date, language we have inherited from our Silicon Valley chums over the water. Many of us might call it 'making it up as you go along' and 'learning from your mistakes'. Is 'Agile' some kind of techie religion, I ask myself? No.

The problem with agile systems is that bigger projects require huge teams and one small change can affect the entire system. Later in this series I will delve into agile as a form of governing and changing public services, but for now suffice to say we need to get the bigger picture.

The Faceless Society is being constructed before us, as health care, benefits and social interaction go online. Our whole lives are now rapidly turning into a series of clicks and swipes. But at the outset we can see that the danger is that mothership digital is gradually opening up a digital divide between the rich and the poor, one where you have things done for you, like online shopping. And one where you have them done to you, like Universal Credit.

Oddly the two examples connect us to a bigger problem, the one of mass automation. I recently wrote about Vocado for *The Image*, a company that is forging ahead on completely automated picking systems for online shopping. I was invited to go to one of their factories in Hertfordshire where a vast warehouse contains miles and miles of tracking systems, dropping your organic rice cakes carefully into bags that then appear at the door. So far they haven't got rid of the driver but they are working on that. My point is, work is changing and 'getting people back into work' as IDJ proposes isn't that simple. The processes of digitisation and automation are moving our society away from the kind of low paid jobs imagined for the working poor and ever further to the precipice of the digital divide. Automation is now shifting the idea of work faster than the work force itself can understand.

I met G4N CEO Barry Hamilton at his offices in London to talk about the roll out of UC and their work in pulling the project back from the brink in terms of service design and back-end hardware. Barry is a charming man with a PR team behind him to obfuscate and disarm the most tenacious of journalists. In fact I was so distracted by them that I had barely anything to write about. G4N has moved the UC programme away from agile as a method and instituted a root and branch overhaul of the IT associated with it. Barry did however give me one golden nugget to play with – "you can't create a welfare system from post-it notes, at some point you have to have an overall design."

What Barry Hamilton is referring to is the need for some form of human engagement to make the whole thing work. At the moment this is not clear, but the tests in places like Bristol are showing where the weak spots lie. How effective will the money management advice offered to claimants be? Landlords accustomed to direct housing benefit payments will get a surprise when tenants find it hard to make choices between paying the rent or the electricity bill. As the Universal Credit pilot continues, stories are coming in of punitive fines being imposed on UC claimants who are in work. Yes, if you work less than 35 hours per week you still need to attend Jobcentre meetings and be actively seeking a second job. We hear of the UC claimant who said she was fined £70 after her work shift meant she arrived late at a Jobcentre appointment. And another in-work UC claimant on a zero hours contract with unpredictable hours which meant he incurred multiple fines for missing appointments and is now facing eviction. That certainly is making work pay, or more correctly perhaps, making you pay for work.

Chapter 4

May

Diane takes the train to Bristol once more. She gazes out of the window as Wiltshire passes by in a blur. A woman and child opposite are playing a game together on an iPad, the child handing the headphones over to the mother every so often for her to have a listen. They take a break from the iPad and tuck into their packed lunch - sandwiches wrapped in foil and bags of salt and vinegar crisps. The smell of the food makes Diane's stomach rubble and she searches in her bag for the half eaten flapjack she'd been snacking on in the tube earlier.

Once she's checked into the hotel, and spurred on by her hunger, Diane calls her friend Kesha in St Pauls. She likes staying with Kesha, but she's been up to Bristol a lot recently and she doesn't want to out stay her welcome. Plus the pull of a fancy hotel was too strong.

"I'm not going to stay with you this time, I've got a budget for a hotel finally and plenty of writing. Are you free for lunch? I've been holding out for a Kino burger and chunky fries," Diane says.

She meets her friend at Cafe Kino in Stokes Croft and they catch up on the latest gossip. Kesha keeps smiling, fiddling with the cutlery, and shifting around in her seat.

"Kesha, you look like you're going to explode. What's going on?" Diane asks finally, unable to cope with anymore shuffling about.

"I'm pregnant!" she beams. "Three months gone!"

Diane is taken aback. "What?....so, then, you were pregnant last time I saw you and you didn't tell me?"

"Yes, sorry. I was dying to tell you, I really was. You are my best bud after all. But I just didn't want to jinx it. You understand, don't you, Auntie Diane?" Kesha says, putting on a big display of puppy eyes, head cocked to one side, smiling.

Diane laughs. "Well rather you than me. All those poopy nappies, broken sleep and baby sick. No but, really, that's great news. I've never been an Auntie."

"And I've never been a mother!" Kesha and Diane look at each other in mock horror, mouths open. "Arrgh!" they chorus together and then start giggling.

"I'm starving. Where's our food?" Kesha asks looking around for a waitress.

"I'll go and ask. And seeing as you're eating for two, I better get us some of that double chocolate chip cake for afters," Diane jokes.

"Us? What's your excuse?" Kesha laughs.

Diane stands up, hand on heart.

"I just want to let you know I'm going to support you in every way I can during your pregnancy, including helping you with large quantities of cake."

Later Diane makes a few calls and summons the energy to think about how she is going to pull the next piece together. She phones round a couple of contacts in the community sector and hears about some work happening over in Easton. Ubuntu Community Centre is giving advice on Universal Credit and offers drop ins for local residents. They also offer business development sessions for people on a low income, and English classes to recent immigrants.

Diane spends the late afternoon scribbling down more notes for the next article. She falls asleep on her hotel bed and wakes at 6.30pm. Feeling hungry she decides to walk out and find some food. Down in the hotel lobby she witnesses three loud men emerging through the main doors and a taxi pulling away. They step aside and let her through. She walks around the harbour side area of the city and gets a falafel from the take away stall at the water's edge.

Craig Tumbleton, Chairman of G4N, welcomes the board to the meeting.

"Thanks all for coming along this afternoon, we do have a busy agenda and some important business to get through. I've invited Barry, whom of course you all know, along to talk to us about the roll out of Universal Credit."

Barry smiles and nods at the faces around the table. He wasn't looking forward to this meeting, some of the board members could be deliberately combative as a way of massaging their own egos. He was surprised to see Harriet Devonshire-Gables. Harriet was the god-daughter of Sir Newton Abbotsley, the owner and editor of the *Daily*

Saliva. A trust-fund socialite, it is unusual for her to make it along to a G4N board meeting, she is usually too busy being photographed at private views and openings. Still having her nominally on the board ensured G4N has some press on their side. Plus Sir Newton throws the most extravagant parties.

“And we also have John Turner with us, head of the G4N housing subsidiary, Red Doors Ltd, which houses asylum seekers. He will be giving us an update on our migrant situation.” Craig continues.

Barry is glad John was there. Things have been going tits up with Red Doors Housing as far as Barry could see, and that might divert some of the attention away from him. That old bugger Don Cox, seated at the end of the table, had a particular bee in his bonnet about 'new communities' ever since his favourite boozer had been turned into a mosque.

“So to item one on our agenda. The roll out of Universal Credit, our key role in its redesign and I think what we are calling a ‘reset’, that’s right isn’t it Barry?” Craig gestures to Barry.

“Yes, Craig, we are performing a ‘reset’ for the DWP with some tight turnarounds but I have my angels on it right now. I am confident that they can expedite a full transition and bring it all back on track within the allocated period,” says Barry.

“Tell us, briefly, Barry, what were the salient points of order and issues that we inherited from others?” Craig asks with irony in his voice.

“We inherited a considerable beast with two rear ends and no head, Craig,” Barry quips.

The room laughs, they’ve become accustomed to Barry’s dead pan humour. “The essential problem with UC and Deep Hole was the adoption of agile development processes by consultants who will remain unnamed,” Barry adds.

“What is agile, Barry?” asks Baroness Sharmi Silver.

Barry likes Baroness Silver. She had been a gold medalist Olympic Equestrian in the 1996 Atlantan Games. She quit horses, became an Olympic ambassador and then set up a food packaging empire which now had an annual turnover of £12 million. She was a fantastic business woman, and, in Barry's opinion, rather charming.

"Agile, or one could say 'making it up as you go along' consists of many small work groups sitting in rooms with post-it notes tackling particular design problems. Eventually the post-it notes go all the way down the corridor and no-one has any idea what is going on," Barry answers.

Again the board laugh.

"But before I go further, I need to talk about life inputs. You will be aware that our current rulers are very keen on the term 'life chances'. They use this in a sophisticated way to describe how we can all direct our own lives and be better people, don't they? Well our fellas have borrowed somewhat from upstairs and they describe data fields in the system as life inputs. It has actually been a helpful vernacular: when we are designing the user side of the project we say to ourselves 'what life inputs do we need and from whom?' So, for example, the applicant might give us a place of birth and the employer might give us some real time data on their gross salary for the month, and both of these are life inputs."

Barry looks around the room to see if he still has the board's attention. Harriet is tapping away on her iPhone and Don Cox appears to be asleep. No great loss.

"Significantly, UC has multiple variables as we are inputting a huge range of life inputs into a database that then has to perform algorithmic magic to determine what people get. In turn the introduction of real time input from employers for their staff adds extra computing tasks to the mix. Of course this avoids under or overpayments commonly associated with Working Tax Credits but it means we have a live system that needs to be able to process all this data. Agile, we have observed, will result in considerable cost over-runs and iteration."

"So, Barry, what will our 'reset' do to obviate these issues?" asks Baroness Silver.

"Our system now has a finite design and over-view, it has pilot stages that we are testing. It has dedicated people working on user experience and back end processing and you'll never guess...they all meet up every week, in person, and discuss progress – no Skype!"

"Thank you, Barry, lucid as ever," says Baroness Silver, with smile.

"Can you give us a brief…and I do say brief…update on UC development, please Barry?" asks Craig.

"Yes, I can, it will work," Barry says and stops.

The laughter from the board this time causes Harriet Devonshire-Gables to look up, albeit briefly, from her phone.

"The software install has gone to Agile Plus 15.9 now. Before you ask, we have kept the old naming system from the previous lot. I won't lie, there have been a few blips and crashes recently. The testing in Bristol has been largely successful and a few claimants have been kept waiting but other than that we could be ready for national roll out in a matter of six months, maybe more, maybe less…" Barry tails off.

Craig flicks through the paperwork in front of him and clears his throat.

"Thank you, Barry. And I see you have prepared a detailed report for us. Has everyone got that?" Craig asks as he looks round the room. "Yes, good. So I suggest we move onto item two on the agenda, Red Doors Housing Ltd."

Barry sits back in his chair. He feels pleased with himself in having charmed his way through the meeting. Now he can sit back and watch John in the hot seat.

"John, can you summarise where we are on this one?" asks Craig.

"Well, everyone knows we had some bad press issues with the doors being repainted on the asylum seekers housing. But this was just down to the batch of Signal Red that we purchased on wholesale from Perkins and Whisper," says John, smiling widely.

"We've only just moved into provision of temporary housing for asylum seekers. The units we are now using to house immigrants were previously rented out by Red Doors to private tenants, and well, having red doors on the houses wasn't a problem then."

"So, John, it didn't occur to our people that there might be an issue with using Signal Red, and therefore singling out the asylum seekers?" Craig asks sternly.

"I have been in touch with our North East office and they have told me that we generally use Signal Red because it matches the Red Doors logo. Similar shade, that kind of thing," John answers.

Barry watches John's discomfort. He is beginning to enjoy the slightly gladiatorial feeling of the board meeting, now he's off the hook.

"I, of course, personally ordered the North East office to go round each house with a colour chart and ask the residents what they wanted. Mostly people were happy with any colour, as long as they didn't have their doors or windows kicked in. So the doors have now been repainted."

"John, I trust we are getting in some PR to smooth over this mistake?" asks the Baroness.

"Yes, Lady Silver, we have Friends PR all over it. They have organised a photo shoot with 'satisfied costumers' in front of their newly painted doors and had a journalist from the *Daily Saliva* interview some of the more sympathetic and photogenic tenants," John answers.

Don Cox, Board member for Quality and Integrity, whom Barry had assumed was still quietly dozing at the end of the table, suddenly chips in. "There have been issues with the quality of the housing as well haven't there, John?"

"Yes, Don, there have, mostly damp and black mould, and some of the heating systems have been failing," says John.

"And what are we doing about that John? We don't want the value of the housing stock to drop, do we?" Don asks. "Some of the areas where we presently house immigrants I would class as up and coming. I was in Butetown in Cardiff the other day. Don't ask me why," Don turns and smirks at Harriet, "and I was able to find a decent latte and gastropub serving a rather decent real ale. A first sign of an area on the up, I say. We may well look at liquidating our assets in those areas if that trend continues. So, as I was saying what are we doing about that John?"

"We have sent a leaflet to all tenants asking them to open their windows to alleviate the problem in the short term, then we will get around to installing roof extractors. We are presently evaluating the New Year budgets and we think it may be possible in Q3. As for the failing heating systems, again we will have to wait until Q3 to assess that, but we have provided each unit without heating with a plug in electric heater," John answers.

"Well, we need to tell them not to turn up their heating too high and open a window don't we?" chips in Harriet Devonshire-Gables, who has been desperately waiting to contribute to the conversation but couldn't really think of anything to say.

"Yes, we do, thank you for your input Harriet," says Craig, with only a tiny trace of condescension in his voice. Harriet beams back, happy to have added to the discussion.

The meeting continues to the next agenda item – finance. The final item on the agenda is diversity.

"Any reports on that one, Charlotte, if you wouldn't mind?" says Craig.

"Yes, we have been asked by the government to report back to them on our diversity at board level," she says. "I have told them that we have Baroness Sharmi Silver as our diversity member. Plus of course there are three women on the board. They have suggested we need another person of colour on the board and I have approached Sir Trevor McDonald, whom I thought would be rather good fun, plus bring us some great press coverage," says Charlotte from HR.

"Well done Charlotte, and if there isn't any other business, I think we can now have lunch," Craig concludes.

There is a clink of a trolley behind them and the sandwiches are brought in. Barry is delighted that he's got through the meeting relatively unscathed.

At the gates of Ubuntu Community Centre, Diane looks over to three Somali children playing on the scooter toys in the garden. There is a patch of bluebells growing randomly out of a decaying wooden tub. A sprawling piece of graffiti covers the front porch of the centre showing people dancing. An italic legend runs across the top of the design – *'Light the Spirit of Humanity Once More!'*

Diane gains entry at the buzzer and says hello to the people in the office on the right. Mariam, the course leader, greets her as she walks round the corner into the main corridor. She leads her to the end room where there are about twelve people, sitting in a circle, chatting in twos and threes. All but one are women.

Mariam insists that Diane sits within the circle and they go round and introduce themselves. She checks that everyone is comfortable with Diane attending as an observer, and then she starts the session.

Mariam has drawn a large circle on the floor with the letters A to H written at cardinal points. She tells them about the exercise that they are about to perform.

"This is a form of what we call transactional analysis. It's basically a way of us finding out more about each other and building an understanding among us," she says.

Diane feels a bullshit detector moment coming on. She wonders what this is all about. Mariam continues and gets everyone to stand up.

"So, if you have a British passport, go and stand at letter 'B'," she says. Half of the participants move to letter 'B'.

"And if you have children move to letter 'C'," she follows up.

After a series of questions to the room, Diane can see that the exercise has checked everyone in to each other's lives. She sees a parallel with the concept of life chances.

Mariam introduces Helen from Communities Count, a voluntary sector organisation offering support to new businesses. Helen begins talking to people about setting up a CIC, a Community Interest Company and how the asset lock works. There is some confusion in the session.

"Can you explain the asset lock and what it is for?" Shireen asks.

"Yes. The asset lock is designed to make sure that any assets that are created are used for the benefit of the community. So, for example if anyone leaves the Community Interest Company, they can't take anything from it, like computers or furniture," Helen clarifies.

"Furthermore, if the CIC folds or winds up, the assets have to go to another CIC or charity, they can't be taken or divided among the people who run it if they are a part of the asset lock," says Helen.

There is still some obvious confusion in the room. "So, we want to set up a jewellery making business, called Life Chances, that benefits ourselves and the community, should we become a CIC, like you say?" Shireen asks.

Life Chances was not a phrase Diane was expecting to hear in this situation. She looks at Shireen with interest.

"Well, you have two options – you can be a simple limited company for profit or a Community Interest Company with shareholders. But, with the CIC, the shareholders can have different levels of shareholding and consequently greater dividends if the company makes any profits. The Directors of the company are therefore involved in a company that can create a certain percentage of profit for themselves and another percentage of benefit for the community."

Helen looks round the group. "Does that all make sense?"

"This is something I've been thinking about for some time. Thanks, your explanation was clear and to the point, I understood it!" says SHE.

Mariam finishes the session with a 'go round' and everyone says they have found it informative. After the meeting, Diane goes over to where Shireen is chatting with SHE.

"Hi, sorry to butt in. Could I chat to you about why you've come along today?"

"We want to set up a community business, making jewellery. But also something more meaningful than that. Somewhere people have an opportunity just to talk, share their stories and skills and start thinking about how to change what's going on for people in our community. To take back some of the power that has been taken from us…" Shireen says.

"We want to do something that benefits us, empowers us and helps us to grow as a community," says SHE forthrightly.

"Well, I'm sure the government would be delighted if you set up a business like this, they're all for entrepreneurship," Diane challenges back.

"We're not doing it for the government, we're doing it for us," says Shireen.

"Yes, exactly," says Diane. "The government want more people to start businesses and then we see less dependency on the state for benefits and services."

There is a silence. SHE knows exactly where this woman is coming from and she doesn't like it.

"I'm a journalist, I'm interested to know why you decided to call your business Life Chances – again that seems very much in-line with the current national thinking," Diane continues.

SHE feels annoyed by Diane's line of questioning. But then this is where it starts she thinks. If they want Life Chances to be a success they're going to need to get some press coverage. But she's not sure if she likes the attitude of this particular journalist.

"I'm interested in following your progress and writing about what happens with your business, can I do that?" asks Diane.

SHE looks at Diane and simply says: "No."

Diane is slightly taken aback, but thanks them for their time and leaves the community centre.

"You were a bit hard on her, tek time, SHE. Wouldn't some press help Life Chances?" Shireen says.

"Yeh, we do need press coverage, but we haffi choose who and when, wi nuh ready yet. And anyway I thought she was a bit too bright. Jamilah knows her and says she's doing a tour round 'deprived Britain'. I don't know about you, but I don't want to be described as 'deprived'. If she's sincere, she'll come back on a different tip. Right now I don't think she would represent us, honestly, as we are."

Diane takes the taxi back to the Bristol Hotel. She feels she has enough to start on her second article. The taxi stops outside the hotel and she decides to have some lunch at the bar. The waiter takes her order and on the table next to her are the same three men she saw earlier, chatting and drinking pints. She overhears them talking heatedly about computer systems.

"Yo, don't sit there on your own eating. Why don't you join us?" Toby, now flying high on four pints of Guinness, exhibits a bravado towards unknown women he doesn't have when sober.

Diane, who unsurprisingly is not interested in talking to pissed-up idiots in bars, is just about to 'politely' decline when she notices the G4N logo on the passes the three men wear around their necks.

"Sure," she says. Toby, unused to his chat up lines actually working, pulls out a chair and Diane sits down. "What are you guys doing in Bristol?" she smiles.

"Well we've been called in to sort out a massive computer system," Toby boasts.

"This is Tungsten, he's the audit man," Toby says pointing to Graham. "This is the man of law, Strontium, sometimes called *Scrotium*" he says pointing to Jeff, who gives him a kick under the table, "and I'm the IT guru, Lithium."

"Tungsten, Strontium and Lithium, interesting... umm... tags." Diane can't quite believe it, but she seems to have bumped into the characters from *The Big Bang Theory*. She decides to play along. If these geeks are from G4N they might have something interesting to say. Possibly.

"So Lithium, what do IT gurus do, then?" asks Diane.

Jeff, equally lubricated after four pints of lager, interjects. "We're a team of fixers and we work for a big firm. When shit happens we get sent out to solve it basically, and right now there's plenty of it."

"Yep, we're like the A-team. I'm not sure which one of us is Mr T, but I'm definitely the Face." Graham slurs slightly as he gets up to order another round. "Wanna drink love?" he asks but staggers off before Diane can answer.

"My main skills are in digging big old IT systems out of their deep holes and putting them back on the interweb of light and soundness," says Toby.

They're like a pack of school boys trying to outdo each other, thinks Diane.

Feigning a lack of knowledge she asks, "oh, I've read about something called 'Deep Hole' in *The Image*."

"Yeh, well that's us, love, we're da Deep Hole fixing crew, ha ha..." Toby boasts.

"What I read in *The Image* and the *Daily Saliva* seems to suggest it's over budget and doesn't work," says Diane.

"To be honest, between me and you, it's all true," says Toby "but we will have it up and running in no time. Our boss gives us a bag full of cash and we get cracking. We've pretty much finished now, which is why we're having this little celebration," Toby says.

Diane can't believe her luck, an inside track from a bunch of sozzled nerds.

"Oh, I don't know anything about computers at all but it seems a big step to shift the whole benefit system onto them," she says again feigning ignorance.

"Damn right it is," says Toby. "We have been here for over a week trying to sort the sodding thing out. But it's not just here we have an entire network to deal with across the country. This is just a pilot system here, bit of a Mickey Mouse version of the real thing."

"Oh, so Deep Hole is everywhere then?" she asks. The three men laugh at what they see as a joke.

"Yes," says Jeff. "Deep Hole is everywhere and it's coming ever closer to you as we speak. Maybe you've seen the tax office posters, love – they are watching you and there's nowhere to hide!"

Diane laughs along with them. She can't decide whether it is sweet or nauseous that they are so keen to impress her. Probably a bit of both. She wonders if the three men in front of her think about the politics behind what they are doing. Building a system that rigidly monitors the working poor, while the working rich seem unbounded in hiding their income through off-shoring. How about a 'real time information' system for the rich operating in a similar fashion where their taxation fluctuates on a monthly basis? This she knows is the true ideological and inequitable reality of partly regulated free market systems – now there's an oxymoron. But how she wonders do you write about something like this and gain an audience?

Diane is reminded of her journalistic training: 'avoid undercover or surreptitious methods of gathering information unless traditional methods will not yield vital information to the public'. But then she checks herself, she has made every effort to engage IDJ, G4N, the government and various departments and they all seem intent on stonewalling the situation with Deep Hole and Universal Credit.

"What do you do, love?" says Toby. "Oh, I work in media," says Diane. She gets up and excuses herself.

"I've got a call booked with my boss, sorry I've got to go, thanks for the chat."

"Oh, leaving so soon? Wanna hook up later for a drink?" Toby asks.

"No. No thanks. I've got some meetings later," Diane replies, looking at her phone.

"Can I take your number then?" Toby momentarily thinks about his girlfriend in London and starts to feel a bit guilty, but he doesn't want to lose face in front of his friends.

"It was great to meet you. Maybe see you at breakfast?" Diane says, ducking the question. 'Lithium' is starting to get as annoying as his nickname.

"Well here's my card, you know, if you feel lonely later..." Toby pulls out a G4N business card out of his back pocket.

Diane looks at the card. "Thanks, Toby. I will bear that in mind. I really will." A touch of sarcasm creeping into her voice. Jeff and Graham start giggling into their pints.

Diane walks out of the hotel and onto the street. She has a bit of time before her interview with Asha, a Somali woman Jamilah has set her up with. The Somali Association isn't far, so she decides to walk and phone Nick on the way. She explains the encounter in the hotel with the three G4N guys.

"Well it sounds to me like they offered up a lot of information without any questioning from you. I can tell you that the NUJ code would see this as overwhelmingly in the public interest as a story. If I were you I'd write up what you have and see if you can talk with them again," he advises, "but you don't have to tell them what you're working on, because we have tried to go down the legit route."

"OK, thanks Nick. Lithium, who turns out to be called Toby, did give me his card, so I'll give him a ring..."

“Where you off to now? You sound like you're outside.” Nick asks.

“I'm on my way to interview a Somali woman about her experience of the welfare system.”

“Great. I like the multi-cultural angle you're going for. You could do some more of that. Let me know how it goes.” Nick replies.

“Yes, thanks. Speak to you later.”

Diane arrives at the Somali centre to find Jamilah and Asha waiting for her. They go into a private room and Diane switches on her voice recorder.

“Thanks so much for meeting with me today, Asha. Can you tell me a bit about your family and your circumstances?” Diane asks.

Asha is a bit uncertain about speaking with a journalist, but Jamilah told her that Diane has written positive articles about the Somali community in the past and she trusts Jamilah. She is feeling so frustrated with what is happening in her life, may be talking to a journalist might help?

“I am a mother, I have five children, my husband Abdi is working. He is a bus driver. We have been here for eight years. Before we came I was a teacher in Somalia, I taught Somali to young children. But I cannot teach here, I do not have the right qualifications and I have my children to look after,” Asha says.

“Do you mind me asking, do you have UK citizenship?” Diane asks.

“This is difficult for me. We both have Dutch citizenship. We spend a lot of money applying for UK citizenship. My husband got his, but my application failed. Something wrong with the paperwork. Now I must apply again, it is so much money, we cannot afford it. I am worried. And now the UK is leaving the European Union...” she trails off.

Asha doesn't like to think back to their flight from Somalia and their journey to Holland. She is scared for her children. What if she has to go back to Holland? With Britain leaving the EU, Holland could easily tell her she is no longer welcome. If she is forced to return to Somalia by herself, what would happen to her children? Would they be able to stay in the UK with her husband Abdi? And what would happen to her? Having fled the violence of the civil war, how would she be treated in

Somalia, as a lone woman who ran away?

"Have you applied for Universal Credit?" Diane enquires.

Asha regains her thoughts. "Yes, I have. First I made a call to the helpline and they told me it was an online system and I have to provide evidence of who I am and where I live. That was in February. It took me a week to get the documents I needed and then I went into the Jobcentre to make the application. I am not so good with computers so I took my son Said with me. We tried but we couldn't finish the form because I didn't have all the figures I needed with me about our income. We couldn't save the form, so we had to do it all again," she says.

"So, what about housing benefit and paying your rent?" Diane asks.

"They told me at the Jobcentre that we would get one amount into a bank account. But I didn't have a bank account, so I opened one. This took two more weeks," she says.

"And did you get the money ok in the end?" Diane enquires.

"Yes, we had to wait six weeks before we could get any money. The other problem is that we had no money coming in apart from my husband's wages and child benefit, so we had to pay the rent from that. Before we got Housing Benefit towards the rent which was paid direct to the landlord, which we wanted to happen still and the council tax too. Because of the wait we did not have enough money to cover all the bills and I had to get a referral to the food bank. I found this very difficult."

Asha pulls her hijab closer around her head. She was so embarrassed when she visited the food bank, especially as her son's school had been collecting donations for the food bank the very week she went there. They had been very kind and she had seen some of her neighbours there, which had made her feel better and more depressed at the same time. It felt like everyone was struggling.

"And were there any other problems or improvements in the system for your family?" Diane asks.

"We had a problem. My husband works different hours each week and our income changes. Sometimes he does extra shifts, sometimes they have too many drivers and he gets different shifts," she adds.

"So how much does your husband earn, if you don't mind me asking."

"He earns £10.45 an hour. Sometimes he works over 50 hours a week," she answers. "Then the money from Universal Credit dropped because he had worked more hours."

"That's the tapering system that kicked in on your husband's earnings and the real time earnings figures from his employer," Diane tries to explain.

"I don't understand those things," sighs Asha, "with five children to look after, and a house to run, bills to pay, it's difficult to get the time to find the right person to give me the correct advice. The helpline is so expensive to call and you always have to wait in a queue. No-one official seems to know what is going on. They just tell you to google everything."

"So what happened next?" Diane asks.

"We got into real trouble because of the delay in getting the first payment, so we did not have enough money coming in. We didn't pay the council tax on time and we are behind on our rent. Then we had a big gas bill," Asha replies.

Diane can see the worry etched into Asha's face. Not only does Asha have to deal with a faulty welfare system which penalises the working poor, she is on the rough end of Brexit. Maybe UK Border Control should change their signage, Diane thinks – *'Welcome to Great Britain. Now fuck off'*.

"I'm so sorry you are having such a tough time," says Diane, feeling she cannot provide an adequate response to Asha's story.

"Insha'Allah," Asha sighs.

They finish the interview and Diane thanks Asha for her time. She gets back to the hotel room and posts the second article to Nick.

Universal Credit and the Deep Hole you may be in

This week on my tour of benefit Britain I've been in Bristol, where things are not what they seem. I've been trying to get under the hood of the new Universal Credit system and find out exactly how it will affect working families. You remember the mantra – 'We want work to pay' – so does it?

As yet, there's no clear answer to this, as the new system continues to roll out across the country. What do we know? There have been huge problems with the system itself and it is massively overspent as a new government project. Many people still have no idea how it will affect them and many more don't understand how it all works. Following on from my last article, the critical thing is going to be 'digital literacy' – the working families and those not yet working will need to get themselves up to speed with the technology pretty sharpish. If you have internet at home then there are a myriad of online tools and assistants, so go and check them out. If not, head over to the Jobcentre or, if you can find one, a library with free computer access.

This week I've spoken to a number of working families in Bristol and I can tell you that the pilot scheme is already looking like a recipe for trouble. Perhaps the biggest shift in practical terms is that lower income families are going to have to get much better at personal income management than they have been in the past. You will remember that under the 'nannying' approach of New Labour many of these benefits could be paid direct to the agencies or bodies involved; like your landlord, housing association or local authority. Not so with UC, as the average working family will need to get out the jars to split the money, or at the very least the accountant in the family will have to be on the ball with money management.

Some of the people I spoke to said they wanted their bank to provide them with better money management tools as the system becomes more electronic. One person suggested a mobile phone app for personal money management linked to their Universal Credit outcome. A point well made, as there are few tools available to assist people with this kind of thing, let alone apps. The government spokesperson I contacted did offer some candid comments though: 'We recognise that moving from the old system to a digital by design one, with a single monthly payment, will result in issues for some claimants. That's why we have developed personal budgeting support to help claimants take greater responsibility for their finances and ease the transition into paid work. Most people do now have mobile phones and we will certainly embrace your idea of thinking about apps and money management tools.'

Looking deeper into the impact of UC, I met with one family who had struggled against the Real Time Information system deployed by the government. This now effectively means that employers send their PAYE information to HMRC, the tax office, which then automatically passes this information on the Department of Work and Pensions (DWP). This is assessed in what they call real time, so in theory, your employer sends HMRC your payroll data at 9am and it can be taken account of in the Universal Credit assessment at the end of the same day. This real time data is sent from HMRC to DWP on a daily basis. Yes, very digital by design, I hear you say. In the case that I encountered the employer had failed to input the correct data in terms of hours, which fed through into earnings in the payroll system which automatically triggered the taper in the system and the family got less than they expected. The result was that the family then had their whole claim put on hold.

I have spoken to a few insiders on the matter of Universal Credit IT roll out. They are the poor souls tasked with sorting out the mechanics and machinations of Universal Credit following the great 'reset' debacle. They tell me that there are still major functional issues with the new system, largely down to scaling up such a huge shift in procedure. All of my attempts so far to gain insights from the Department of Work and Pensions and G4N have met with failure, so I was delighted to happen upon these helpful G4N IT insiders in a bar (yes these things do happen!). To preserve their anonymity I won't mention any names, but it was clear in our conversation that the present corporate strategy is to bluster through on PR, remember work does pay, and to fix the damn thing as fast as possible. However, digital by design means the following - you have to plug in all of your data, six weeks are disregarded as a waiting period, the DWP has to process your data, they then have to send a message to mark you on the system at the tax office, your employer has to provide the real time data and then you get Universal Credit in your bank account. Oh, and it's paid monthly in arrears. And even when you are in the system you may be paid wrongly or unpredictably, as in the case already mentioned. Yet we are told that this is a more efficient process.

Toby's mobile rings as they are about to leave the hotel and head back to London. "Toby, it's Barry, have you seen the article in *The Image*?" says Barry.

"Barry, you know I don't read newspapers. Why what is it?" answers Toby.

"It's on their website, Toby! I've taken a few calls from Friends PR and they say the article is written by Diane Butler, the same woman who came here to my office. She met some 'helpful G4N IT insiders' in a bar, for god's sake, and they blabbed about Deep Hole and how unworkable it is. So Toby, I'm assuming she's talking about you, Jeff and Graham. What the fuck is going on?" Barry asks angrily.

Toby realises that he is well and truly in trouble and tries to figure out some kind of response.

"We haven't spoken to anyone, chief, we've been stuck in various server rooms and audit offices looking at procurement," he replies.

Jeff and Graham look at Toby, puzzled, their heads thumping from what turned into a mammoth drinking session yesterday.

Barry is extremely angry and threatens to fire Toby.

"If I didn't need you Toby, you'd be history, now just keep your mouth shut and get back to London asap," Barry shouts down the line and hangs up.

"Whoops," Toby grins at his cohorts.

The three G4N fixers get in the taxi and head towards Temple Meads Station. Toby's mobile rings again. "Hello, it's Derek, is that Toby?" says Derek in the G4N Bristol office.

"What's the crack, bruv?" Toby asks.

"I need you to come back, Toby. Deep Hole is making an odd groaning noise. I know this sounds daft, but it kind of sounds like a wounded animal..." replies Derek, feeling a bit foolish. Desiree had told him it had been making noises, but he hadn't believed her. Turns out she was right.

360
360

Chapter 5

June

Mariam is meeting with Desiree, SHE and Shireen at Ubuntu to help them with their business plan. It's 25 degrees outside and it's hot and stuffy in the community centre. Mariam nips out of the meeting room to get one of the air-conditioning units the centre has had to buy as the architect who designed the building failed to get the ventilation right. Plus the windows on the first floor only open a crack, just in case someone fancies jumping out.

Mariam bumps into Diane as she's making her way back. "I didn't expect to see you today. I haven't forgotten you were coming have I?" Mariam asks.

"We did talk about me coming along to your Tuesday one-to-one sessions with your budding entrepreneurs. We didn't firm anything up, but I'm in Bristol for my friend's baby shower, so I thought I'd drop in on the off chance. Is that ok?" replies Diane.

Whilst Mariam likes Diane, she is wary of journalists. She's been a community activist for over thirty years and she knows how the press can twist things to fit their agendas. But she thinks Diane's interest in what they are trying to achieve at Ubuntu might be useful, and she knows the women she is working with at the moment are no fools.

"Well it's ok with me, but you'll have to get the ok from SHE, Shireen and Desiree, who I'm meeting with at the moment. I'm not sure SHE took to you very well last time."

Mariam and Diane walk into the meeting room. "What are you doing here?" SHE says.

Mariam can see Diane finds SHE's slightly abrasive way of talking challenging. That's what she likes about SHE, she doesn't let anyone get away with anything.

"Hi, sorry. I know we didn't really hit it off last time we met. Would I be able to sit in on your session with Mariam. I'm really interested in the business you're hoping to set up," Diane says.

SHE flashes a look at Shireen and Desiree. They have talked about Diane and decided if she did come back that they should use her interest to further their aims. They'll need to get the word out to a wider audience if they're going to have any chance influencing the decision-makers.

"We're not hoping to set up, we are going to set it up," SHE says, looking Diane up and down. "You can sit in on this one."

Mariam starts a discussion with the women about what they want to achieve. They want to create a safe space for people to engage in wider thinking about how, why and who has power over their lives and then how to take back some of that power. Mariam is excited by their ideas to combine social enterprise with grass roots politics.

"I'm not an expert in this area but there are pots of money targeted at projects like this, where community empowerment has been identified as a priority. I know UnLtd has some grant schemes going at the moment that would fit," Mariam says.

Mariam asks them to write a 150 word summary of what they will do, imagining that they are trying to explain it to someone who knows nothing about them.

The three women work in the corner of the room and Diane asks Mariam about the scheme she is running.

"We have adopted a flexible approach to meet the needs of the huge variety of people we have in the surrounding community. We believe in people, that is the main thing. We see them as the agents of change not the subject of systems. We encourage everyone to push themselves a little bit beyond their safe area. That's it really. I've been working and living in this community for a long time and I've seen a lot of government schemes come and go. The schemes that work are the ones that have actually asked people what they need and then give them to tools to get on with it. And those ones, unfortunately are a rarity."

"Is it ok if I take notes?" Diane asks as she gets her pad and pen from her bag. Mariam nods.

"We have people on the streets dealing drugs and other people manufacturing them in huge automated factories. Of course one is illegal and the other legal, but a lot of this is arbitrary when in fact they are both running businesses aren't they?" says Mariam.

"The government wants people to run businesses don't they? What we see as a middle space is the opportunity to reinvest in people and their communities," she continues.

"This does sound a bit Utopian though doesn't it?" Diane replies. "Are you saying that more people should get into drug dealing?"

"Well of course I'm not, I'm just making a point about how regulation places certain things in a lawful space and other things not," Mariam sits forward in her chair. She enjoys a good political back-and-forth.

"So, can you give me your opinion of what life chances actually mean to everyday people?" Diane asks.

"Yes I can," says Mariam. "Karl Marx talks about the ownership of the means of production. Now we have soft power in terms of ownership of the language of lives, as if each individual is a living unit of production."

"Well they are, aren't they?" says Diane.

"This is the fundamental point isn't it? I could write a whole book on this one. You can increase someone's life inputs and then affect their life chances dramatically. But we don't have an even playing field, do we? The one thing that I find turns shy Tories into thinking democrats is this..." she takes a deep breath, "it is the matter of risk and personal risk. If I am on a zero hours contract and I am dependent on Universal Credit to do all the right things, like care for my family, save a personal pension and buy my own house – exactly how can I carry on without any safety net? My circumstances mean I have maximum insecurity and progressing through the workforce is actually only possible where I mitigate risk through support and encouragement from others. But if I am the daughter of a stockbroker or a wallpaper company owner, many of my life chances come from the relative affluence around me. Risk is always mitigated by a network of safety nets," she stops and then continues."Under Margaret Thatcher we had a breakaway from the state structures and problems of unionisation. She wanted the masses to take some ownership of their life chances didn't she? But the steady dismantling of the state, which is still happening today, has never brought about equality in this country in terms of life inputs. The establishment controls the language used to pin down the poor, through the media and through policy. The shy Tories at home, reading their *Daily Saliva*, are drip fed stories reinforcing a judgmental and contemptuous attitude towards the poor. By controlling the centre ground, people like IDJ are in fact controlling the agenda."

Mariam pauses. "Sorry I know I'm ranting."

"No, please, carry on," Diane replies.

"The middle classes form a buffer between the super-rich and the detached poor. They join in with the finger pointing by proxy through being uninformed about the reality of what's right in front of us."

"So, are you saying that the life inputs of the poor are controlled by the language of the political classes?" Diane asks.

"If we take a system like Universal Credit, what I'm saying is that it has been designed by the political establishment and not by fully representative and democratic involvement of those whom it will affect," answers Mariam.

"But how can the poor or working poor, whatever you call them, be expected to design grand systems of the state?" Diane asks.

"Well that is a very good question, Diane. We believe that low-income families in communities like ours have skills and capabilities that aren't usually recognised by regulatory systems. Such families can be ignored when policy-makers design policy and practice, even when those policies have an direct impact on those families. This needs to change because those policies can only be effective if they are informed by the real lives of those families. Far from raising people out of poverty the new UC system redefines 'in work poverty', emphasising the rhetoric of the deserving and undeserving poor to reinforce the message. The consequence of this new precarity, as it is being termed, is to ensure and enshrine the continuing struggle of the working poor. And the idea of attending coaching classes and money management sessions is a crass form of tutelage of neo-liberal values in a controlled environment," Mariam argues.

"But where is the labour movement in this grand debate?" Diane asks.

"The labour movement is finished and not even represented in the lives of the working poor. People like me are arguing for a whole new economics with people at the centre and increased power to communities through collective action and personal development," says Mariam.

Diane is impressed by Mariam's passion but sees a disconnect between what she is saying and the reality of the surrounding community that they are in.

"This all sounds good, Mariam, but isn't there a bit of history repeating itself here, you know, like a seventies co-op movement reinventing itself?" Diane probes further.

"Well, I will join you, Diane, in the privilege of political hindsight, but I will say that the period between 1997 and 2017 in Britain will be seen as one where the Blair government applied the free market ideas of Thatcher to the centre ground. Subsequent governments then sought control over the same ground, refining and diminishing the state. That is my view...but the casualties all along have been those who have never gained access to the comforts of the middle ground," Mariam argues firmly.

Diane looks toward the three women who are still deeply immersed in talking about their Life Chances project.

"Can I ask you, Mariam, what is realistic as an outcome if you project the life inputs of people on your course over the next few years?" Diane asks.

"What we are doing with scant resources in this room is demonstrating that enterprise and society are really connected and that is where we can leave Thatcher in the past," Mariam answers.

"So, it is possible to give people a life chance?" asks Diane.

"Yes, we are doing that right here and right now," Mariam says.

Secnach and Debra are sitting together in the shade of the cherry trees, outside the social services office, eating their lunch. They can hear the clacking of the commuter trains on the tracks in the distance, and the fut fut fut sound of a lawn sprinkler somewhere to their right.

Debra asks Secnach about Zantonica.

"What's it like then, it looks quite idyllic, from what I saw on Instagram?" Debra asks.

"Because the islands sit between Yemen and India, they were part of the old trade route from India to the African continent. The islands have a history as a stopping off point for traders. Now of course it is a stopping off point for European holidaymakers and it is changing rapidly. Europeans want places to go that no-one else has been to, so Zantonica gives them that. As a people, we are used to change and responding to our visitors, but we have also put policies in place to protect the island from over-development," Secnach says.

Debra takes another bite of her cheese and pickle sandwich and nods her head at Secnach to continue.

"It is very different to Britain. The people have to work together and form close communities. We have learnt from the surrounding dominant cultures that we have to form our own values and systems. The English and the Dutch came during the trading wars and they of course had a major impact on who we are; but we have fought hard to create and maintain our own identity. Because when you create a political system or even social work concepts you have to have something to refer to in terms of values."

Debra is impressed with Secnach's articulate way of describing her homeland.

"I'm not sure there's much you can learn from being here, Secnach." Debra offers Secnach a nectarine, flown in from South Africa.

"Ah, thank you. I have learnt so much already. I feel that one of the main problems facing social services in Bristol is how to construct practices that respond to different cultural backgrounds."

"What do you mean?" Debra asks.

"Well for example. You are a white person and you quite commonly deal with black families. I have seen that this causes problems," Secnach bites into the nectarine.

Debra feels confronted and put out by the comment, but she has warmed to Secnach and is genuinely interested in her opinion.

"Can you give me an example?"

"Yes I can. In your practice you use assertion and mirroring techniques in your work that arise from a Western sociological perspective. In Zantonica this would not work because people there have different body language. It is common for younger people not to make eye contact with their elders, but this is out of respect for them and not because they are guilty or disconnected," Secnach says.

Debra feels annoyed but at the same time wants to know more.

"In our islands we are always moving towards collective action and community, we are not so individualistic. When I have been in client sessions with you I can see that your approach is misunderstood by people and they are suspicious of you," Secnach says.

"Perhaps you might give me some credit though," Debra says, "I've been doing this for 20 years and I have a lot of experience. We have had sessions on culture and diversity on our professional social work courses, and the council sometimes runs equality training."

"I am sorry Debra, I don't mean to be rude. Maybe the training needs to be overhauled? Maybe members of the community you serve need to be involved in the writing and delivery of this training? Then social workers can really work with the cultural values of your clients and see the world from their point of view. It would help them to understand the roles of the oppressor and the oppressed."

Debra goes quiet and looks at her watch. Will does not have much truck with anti-oppressive practice, Debra thinks, he's more worried about managing risk.

"We'd better get off to see the next lot now," she says.

Diane travels to Cardiff on the train to meet Phil and Jonathan at Dragon Welfare. They have been contacted by the Welsh Assembly about ways to connect people positively in Cardiff and to tackle head on the issue of racial tension towards migrants and asylum seekers.

Diane meets them at Phil's place just off Ninian Park Road. "Cup of tea, Diane? No sugar, isn't it?" asks Phil.

They sit and drink tea. Phil listens as Jonathan talks about the opportunity.

"As part of devolution, they are asking us to contribute to 'Dragon 360'. We are always a bit sceptical with these kind of things, you know, we've seen plenty of failed schemes with heady objectives in this area," Jonathan says.

Diane starts writing some notes. This Dragon 360 to her sounds like business speak and advertising agency spin. "So, what have they told you, Jonathan, about this Dragon 360 thing?" she asks, not concealing her own scepticism.

"Unlike schemes before this, Dragon 360 will be led by 'community champions', who will shape the procedures and processes of the scheme. We are told that Dragon 360 is a new way of integrating communities and getting people working together. There will be twenty sessions right the way across the city, for all to attend. We've been asked to host one at Northside too," Jonathan replies.

"Getting the community to shape the project is a great idea of course. But how do you stop the 'usual suspects' from taking over, and do people actually have the time and interest to get involved in something like this?" Diane asks.

"I think you'll be surprised, Diane, by the amount of interest there is in this community in taking back some power over their lives. Cardiff's demographic is in a state of flux and by taking the initiative now, we can work with both the indigenous and new communities. As for the usual suspects, well that's an easy insult to throw at community organisations, but in our case that's not what happens. We are always working to ensure we are reaching out to all parts of the community," Jonathan answers, slightly annoyed.

"Yes, sorry Jonathan, I didn't mean to offend you," Diane says.

"That's ok, I know you don't really mean it. It's just that I think this scheme could actually do something." He looks at his watch. "We better get a move on if we're going to catch Hadi at Northside. She's doing one of our English classes there and I think it finishes around 2.30."

Diane and Jonathan head off, talking more as they walk.

They arrive towards the end of the lesson, and slip in at the back of the room and take a seat.

"I have already spoken to Hadi, and she has agreed to speak to you, in confidence, after the lesson has finished." Jonathan whispers to Diane. "And her friend Amna may also be up for to talking to you, but I haven't had a chance to ask her yet."

Jonathan nods over to where Hadi and Amna are sitting. The teacher clears his throat loudly.

"Ok class, we're going to finish the session by looking at food and cooking. If you can look at this week's handout and turn to page 11, we'll start with ordering food and drink in a pub, a favourite

British pastime, ho, ho."

The teacher admits a short laugh at his own joke, his smile faltering with the realisation that most of his students probably don't frequent public houses. "Though of course it's not something a lot of you will be doing in your lives, going into pubs, but, you know, erm, it might be useful, if at some point, erm in the future, should you change your, erm... Anyway, let's give it a go shall we?"

Amna looks at Hadi and rolls her eyes, whispering to her friend, "he is so young. Looks same age as my Sameer."

All around people are rustling pieces of paper. Amna flicks through her handout and finds the right page by following Hadi beside her. The sheet is full of cartoon images of strange looking food and people with happy faces, drinking.

The teacher starts to read from the sheet.

"Repeat after me. Two pints of lager and a packet of crisps please."
"Two pints of lager and a packet of crisps please," comes the response.

Amna looks round at the visitors that have just sat down at the back. She recognises Jonathan, but not the woman next to her. She hears the woman say something about Ramadan to Jonathan, who in turn nods and looks unhappy.

"I would like the roast beef and Yorkshire pudding please."

"I would like the roast beef and Yorkshire pudding please," Amna chants, unsure as to what she has just said, but enjoying the rhythm of the words.

"How much is the steak and kidney pie please?"

"How much is the steak and kidney pie pleassse?"

The group follows the teacher's intonation, ending the sentence on a long drawn out "Pleeasse." Hadi catches Amna's eye and starts to giggle. Amna smiles.

"This beer is flat. I would like another one, please"

"This beer is flat. I would like another one, pleeassse."

Hadi teases out the 'pleeeassse' even longer and Amna has to cover her mouth to stifle a laugh.

Amna is so glad to have met Hadi. She makes the monotonous call and response of the English lessons fun and it is good to have another woman to talk to, even if they sometimes struggle to understand what each other are saying.

"Right, Ok. Let's do some work in pairs. Turn to page 12. One of you can be the waiter and the other the customer."

Jonathan takes the opportunity to beckon the teacher over. "A word Mr Noakes, please."

Amna and Hadi look at each other and start laughing again. It did Hadi good, goofing around at the class. She was struggling to stay positive after she had been moved again by Red Doors Housing. They were so far from Ayla's school now. It was a long journey each morning and afternoon on public transport and the extra cost meant she had to skip meals sometimes. And the flat was so damp. But she had little choice. Sometimes she worried if she had done the right thing, coming to the UK. But she had to keep her children safe. And they were safe, she told herself. At least they were safe.

"OK. I'm waiter, you customer," Hadi tells Amna. "OK. Umm. How much pleasse," Amna asks.

"How much for what, madam?" Hadi replies.

"How much food?" Amna queries.

"Oh lots of food, madam. We have lots and lots of Yorkshire pudding," Hadi jokes. "You must ask how much for one thing, not all food!"

"Oh yes. I am sorry waiter. How much for Yorkshire pudding in your beautiful restaurant?" Amna says, gesturing around the magnolia walls and grey lino floor of the classroom.

Hadi starts giggling again. Amna always makes her laugh.

"Your necklace, Hadi. It's new?" asks Amna.

"No, I make it back home. You like it?" Hadi replies.

"It is beautiful," Amna looks closely at the intricately woven copper and beads.

"I come round your flat some time. I show you how to make it. I make many jewellery in my home country," Hadi touches her necklace and rolls one of the beads in her fingers.

"Yes please," Amna smiles.

The teacher starts talking. "Right class. I'm sorry, I must apologise. I had no idea it was Ramadan and that some of you will be fasting. So it was wrong of me to include a lesson on ordering food and drink. And of course, as Jonathan has also pointed out, many of you do not drink alcohol and are unlikely to go into a pub. I am truly sorry and I hope I haven't offended anyone," Mr Noakes smiles nervously at the class. "So I think we'll leave it there for today. See you next week, erm, hopefully." He turns off the over-head projector and starts collecting up the worksheets.

Jonathan gets up and motions to Hadi and Amna to come over.

Jonathan introduces Diane to Hadi and Amna. "This is the journalist I was telling you about Hadi. Are you still up for being interviewed now?"

"Yes, it's fine. But I must go in half hour to pick up my daughter," Hadi smiles.

"And Amna, we will talk with Diane another time, when Mahnoor is here and can translate?"

"Mmm, yes?" replies Amna.

Hadi and Amna say their goodbyes and then Diane, Jonathan and Hadi go into the now empty classroom to talk.

"So Diane, Hadi is happy to talk to you as long as everything is anonymous," Jonathan pulls out a chair and sits down.

"Yes of course. I will need to make some notes though, is that ok Hadi?"

"Yes is fine" replies Hadi.

"Can you tell me how and why you came to the UK?" Diane asks

"I arrived at St Pancras on the train. I came from Turkey in 2014. I leave quickly because of the situation there. People were after me," Hadi says.

"What people?" Diane asks.

"People after me and my family, we unsafe there. We had to leave," she replies. Diane wonders who these people might be.

"I went to Police station and I told them I need help, it was somewhere in London. The Police officer shouted at me, he said 'Not another one' and I felt afraid. He sent me to immigration centre in Croydon. I had some money and I got taxi there. I waited for four hours, my daughter she gets upset, there were lots of other people there. All waiting. A man come and take me into a room. He ask me lots of questions and take my photograph. He want to know where I came from and why I want asylum. I told him about being unsafe in my country," Hadi says.

Diane writes it down in her notebook. She can't quite make out the entire story and realises there are elements that probably won't be forthcoming.

"I was given an ID card," Hadi continues.

She shows Diane the card and it says 'FORBIDDEN FROM TAKING EMPLOYMENT' on it. It's similar to the one Mona had in Bristol.

"I given a hostel address in Croydon and we go there and have food. There were lots of other people there from over the world. Then we got moved to Liverpool but I feel unsafe there. We then told we have to go to shared house in Cardiff, Red Doors Housing. We there for six months but then Red Doors Housing say we have to move again, just now, to a flat far from Ayla's school. My older daughter Ezra, she here in UK already. I send her here in 2013. It was dangerous for her then, in my country. She older than Ayla, and now at university." Hadi pauses to take a sip of the water Jonathan has just brought in from the water cooler in reception.

"I'm afraid I not get asylum, I can't go back home, it's too dangerous for me and my daughters. I have another interview at immigration centre, they say that asylum has not been granted and I need more evidence," Hadi continues.

"What evidence do you need?" Diane asks.

"I need to prove to them that what I say is true," says Hadi.

Hadi tells Diane that she receives some money from the state, but it is barely enough to survive. Her daughter is now in school, learning Welsh and English and doing well. She says she has good qualifications and wants to work in Cardiff.

The interview ends as Hadi has to collect Ayla from school. Diane and Jonathan talk about what Hadi has said.

"This is a common thing we see with refugees," says Jonathan, "the system is so complex and people can only make claims and get interviewed in certain cities. They also get passed around all over the country to get housing and we only just about understand the whole system ourselves."

Nick calls Diane on her way back from Northside.

"Diane, Ernst Negri is going to be on the Robin Preston show on Sunday. Are you still in Cardiff? We are pretty sure he will talk with Preston about unconditional credit and basic income guarantee," says Nick.

"Ok, Nick, thanks for the tip, I'll still be here on Sunday and I'll watch it. I've just done this interview with a woman who is seeking refuge in the UK. I'm thinking of working something in on the life chances articles on immigration, what do you think?" she says.

"Go for it, we've had really good feedback from readers on the 'Faceless Society', people love the idea. Just push it in any direction you like but keep moving around, the journey is the thing people are in to. Well done!" Nick enthuses and immediately hangs up.

Diane feels slightly odd, Nick's enthusiasm upsets her. She decides to phone him back.

"Nick, can I be honest with you, this is about life chances isn't it for you? And not some cheap poverty tours UK number?" she spurts out.

"Diane, don't worry, it doesn't come across like that, I can feel you are truly concerned about the issues you are uncovering. Just keep doing what you're doing. I am right behind you." The line goes dead. She wonders if Nick is aware he has an extremely annoying habit of ending calls abruptly.

The following day Diane visits Phil again. She likes his slightly oblique way of viewing things and his authentic way of handling situations. On both sides of the social divide there is a kind of mannered way of doing things. It's like they are reading verbatim from web tool kits on how to do things. She thinks about Kesha talking about reading 'What to Expect, When you're Expecting' the month by month guide for pregnant women. She imagines 'What to Expect, When you Enter the UK'. A smile crosses her face.

On arrival Phil announces that Najma, the North African doctor, has been accepted on the Welsh Assembly funded Dragon 360 programme of support.

"So, she will get some language support, an introduction to the Welsh way of life and then they will evaluate what else needs to be done. She can then progress to stage 2 and they will help her get the qualifications she needs to work as a doctor, and fund the costs, only to be repaid, interest free, once she gets employment. That's great news isn't it?" Phil says.

"This all sounds a bit costly, Phil."

"When the local bean counters do their sums they've added up the cost of keeping her on the state with her and her child on benefits and then looked at the investment in getting her into a much needed post. So it actually saves money in the long term. If it works, Dragon 360 is quite a breakthrough. It's extremely hard to get politicians to think and act in the long term, when they are bedded down into five yearly terms." he says.

Robin Preston chats across the table to Ernst Negri just before going live on "Preston Meets…" Negri, a large man in his late 50's with a clichéd professorial look of goatee beard and glasses, sits in the chair and seems relaxed with Preston's eagerness and jumpy style.

The producer indicates the going live signal to Preston and counts down on his raised fingers to him. The music ends and Robin Preston introduces the discussion for the show.

"On this…weeks…show…we have the eminent and, may I say, sometimes maligned future-social philosopher… Professor Ernst Negri.

He is most well known for his revision and work on the theory of the social contract, which has been published in 15 different languages and more recently he has turned his attention to the issue of basic income guarantee and artificial intelligence. Now for some of us, including, may I say so, myself, there is an evident blue mile of water between the two. However, Professor Negri has been stirring and making waves in this…err…blue mile of water for the last few months. He has recently published the book 'Small is the new BIG'... err…and in today's show we are going to find out a little bit more on this."

Robin Preston turns and smiles at his guest, "Welcome, Professor Ernst Negri."

Negri nods his reply.

"So basic income guarantee or BIG, is a non-means tested state income paid to everyone regardless of their financial circumstances. Richard Branson would be paid the same amount as, say, Bob, who cleans Branson's London penthouse." says Preston, smiling to camera. "It's not a new idea and it's also one that has been trailed in other countries, such as the USA and Canada. What Professor Negri looks at in his book is the urgency of introducing BIG in our automated near future."

Preston turns and looks at his guest. "Professor Negri, how will people work in the future?"

"I imagine a film following a series of robots in a factory. The first robot cuts the sheet of metal from the bale and flattens it. The second robot places it in the stamping device and then removes it. The third robot drills holes in it and then it passes it to the fourth robot who places it inside the evolving car. The fifth robot then sprays it, let's say red and then here we have the first appearance of a man, who will check the metal plate is in the correct place. In the robot factory, if I make this film over and over again in time, the man will come in later in the film until he is completely gone. We are nearing that time now. The human is at the very end of the production line, almost redundant. And soon he will not drive the car either. He will merely sit inside that car made by robots and request to be driven to a leisure park in Los Angeles. In the future the factory will be only robots, no people. But the haircut, Mr Preston, that is difficult to replicate with a machine. Mr Preston you are, for example, unlikely to go to have your hair cut by a robot, is this the case?" Negri asks.

"Yes, I have my hair cut by a hairdresser," Preston responds.

"Well, yes of course, a man will cut your hair, Mr Preston. There are some skilled jobs that will remain in place, even in 2050, but we cannot all be barbers or in my case, philosophers, Mr Preston can we? I cannot, Mr Preston, out-source your haircut to China for example, not easily can I? But on the other hand, your job of presenting a topical news show could be undertaken by an artificial intelligence capable of machine learning," Negri continues.

Preston laughs to camera and is about to reply, but Negri carries on regardless.

"So, the changes in the labour force, the movements of capital, along with globalisation will eventually mean that people will need some income from their political masters to take the robot car to the leisure park. The corollary of artificial intelligence and robotics is, Mr Preston, the necessity for fixed income from the state, a basic income guarantee." Negri asserts.

"I must admit I'm slightly affronted that you think a robot could do my highly skilled and professional job of talking to a camera, Professor Negri," Preston laughs. "But please do continue."

"Thank you, yes, I will. A hundred years ago Henry Ford reduced the manufacture of a car to 84 steps with many men surrounding the car placing the parts on the car. We estimate maybe 140 men were involved in each car. Mr Ford then developed the $5 work day and attracted workers from all over the world to what became a highly paid job. This created a stable work force and a gradual development of the middle classes. One hundred years later, nearly all of those 140 men have been replaced by robots and machines, Mr Preston. There are perhaps one or two men pressing buttons on computers. So, we see in our economies now that these kind of jobs are gone. And we can argue of course, Mr Preston, that there is a limited demand for hairdressing and so we cannot all become hairdressers. Automation and robotics will exponentially increase over the next 50 years and I have called this 'Negri's Law'," Negri says, unflinching in this obvious display of ego.

"So, Professor Negri, how does basic income guarantee fit with automation?"

Professor Negri shifts his considerable weight in his chair. "Well Mr Preston, you see if people don't work then no-one has any money to buy the things made by the robots. There would be a massive slump in aggregate demand if they don't have any income to be consumers."

"But how will this work and who will pay for it? Surely, we can't in this country raise sufficient funds to pay 70 million people a basic living wage for nothing in return?" Preston probes.

"Essentially Mr Preston you have asked me two questions. Number one, what is BIG. Well, this would be a payment from the state to every citizen in the country, irrespective of whether they work or not and irrespective of how much they earn. So payments would be unconditional and not means-tested, unlike Universal Credit. For people on the left of the political spectrum this is about security of income, tackling poverty and promoting equality. For the right, who advocate a similar negative income tax scheme, their aims are to increase personal freedom by reducing state interference.

Number two is how we pay for it. Well, of course if there are fewer people in work we won't have the same tax base as now because they won't have the money to pay tax. But the companies who are using robots and artificial intelligence, they may have higher profits so we could tax them more than we do now. That would only be fair. Those on the left may like this approach because it could reduce inequality by taxing wealth more highly. Others may be persuaded by the fact that this would also bring capitalism back to a more sustainable footing." Negri pauses briefly to drink some water.

"Another idea about how to pay for BIG comes from Alaska, where oil revenues have been put into a fund that then pays out an annual amount to each Alaskan – in effect re-distributing the resources from environmental exploitation to each citizen. We could do something similar in the UK with proceeds from energy and utility companies, or maybe a fracking levy."

Preston grins.

"So," continues Negri, "I would advocate a 'wealth fund' made up of these levies and taxes, which could over time pay for a BIG scheme. There would also be some savings from simplifying the current tax and benefits system, depending of course on the specifics of BIG design."

"But Professor Negri, isn't this all rather Utopian? It's not 'real-politick', surely?"

"Mr Preston, the problem today is that politicians make their calculations on a three, maybe five year cycle at best – when in fact we need planning right now for the next twenty years. Basic income guarantee is not a vote winner in this current climate, but I believe it is necessary and inevitable and will be upon us sooner than we imagine." Negri asserts more strongly this time.

"Could you put a finer figure on that for us?" asks Preston.

"It is always unwise to try and predict the future Mr Preston, but I would say by 2050 there will be an over-supply of people to jobs and this will result in radical changes in welfare," Negri responds. "BIG is the future and we cannot afford to continue living in the past."

"Thank you Professor Negri, I'm sure you've given our viewers a lot to think about."

Toby and colleagues are finally on the train back to London. Derek's worries about Deep Hole were totally fixable and Toby is bathing in a renewed sense of his own importance.

Over the phone, Toby makes sure Barry understands his brilliance.

"Well, I pulled the RTI from the system temporarily and re-patched the script. Total down time on the system, two hours. All sorted for you, Barry."

"Fine. Great. I'm glad to hear you're doing your job." says Barry, heavy with sarcasm.

"I want you to come straight to my office and meet with me and Jem, the ministry are getting jumpy," Barry says firmly.

"I grok, mein frock," says Toby.

"For gods sake Toby, don't be such a twat. Just get your arse down here pronto." Barry hangs up.

Toby arrives at the office looking like he's just returned from a rock festival. Jem disapproves of him and even Barry is starting to rethink his mantra of 'hiring the best people, not the best dressed people'.

"In my job as special adviser to the Secretary of State, I have to keep him well informed of progress on Deep Hole. In particular I want to know exactly when we can expect this to be rolled out nationally, any thoughts on that?" Jem asks Toby.

"Preference, right now, if I'm straight with you, is for staged roll out, no 'go live' day nationally," Toby answers.

"And why is that?" Jem asks.

"Well, in the grand scheme of things we can establish stability and scale, smoothing as we go. We can also avoid a disaster like we just had in Bristol with too many data streams crashing the system," Toby points out.

Barry notes that Toby seems to lose the geek speak when talking to Jem.

"I might add that we also know from the pilot areas that the 42 day turn-around from claim to payment is unviable for claimants... and when we carried out the audit we found a team of fifteen people manually printing out applications and processing them from one system to another," Toby adds.

"Let me be clear Toby, we want you to fix the bloody computers and not have an opinion on the payment timescale. We want a design for an 'end state system' as written into the contract. The manual processing thing, well that must go no further than this room. If word leaks out we're doing that, then all our 'digital by design' PR will be out the window," says Jem.

"But if you want it up and running sooner you may have to have a few more teams printing forms out and entering them back onto the system, seriously..." says Toby.

"Toby, what resources are needed to get to full roll out in six months – that is the 'end state system' not a manual fix?" Barry asks.

"You may need to bring more stuff 'in-house' at the DWP, because the cost over-runs from the first iteration are eye-watering, that would leave G4N consulting on the phased roll-out up until 2020. I don't need to tell you guys that the previous abandoned contract had four corporations all drinking at the trough with no cohesion in the project management – that is until we came along." says Toby.

Barry doesn't like the sound of this at all and Jem is looking nervous. "The audit also revealed invoices being signed off with no apparent knowledge of what was being procured or where it was. This was done by relatively junior staff, not lead officers," Toby adds.

"We haven't asked you to do a financial audit, Toby, what we want is a updated plan on what needs to be done to roll out UC asap," says Jem.

"Fine. The user experience design is not adequate, while the back end IT is gradually stabilising. So we have a system that works in pilot form but the people in the frontline, the Jobcentres and the Citizens Advice Bureaus don't really have a clue how to contact people in the front end office to sort out problems and of course contribute valuable feedback. So, there is evident frustration. I don't think it can be done..." Toby answers.

Jem gets up out of his chair, places his hands on the table and leans close in to Toby's face. Toby automatically moves back.

"That's not want I want to hear Toby. I want you and your overpaid orange team of socially maladjusted geeks to get on with it and get it fucking sorted!"

Jem stands back and looks down at Toby. "Alright?"

Diane writes her third article sitting in a quiet cafe just off the Edgware Road in London.

Human, All Too Human

Last time I wrote about Universal Credit and the roll out issues the new system faces. In this article I am going to drill down into the core of the Life Chances agenda at government level and the contradictions of our brave new digital world. On my journey I have encountered immigrants and asylum seekers, whose life chances are no less affected by the political tides at work in Britain. Indeed, the 'landing strips' or places of relocation for migrants are of course usually located in the poorer areas of this country. This is of course not without problems and consequences; where the indigenous 'working poor' are being asked to budge up, make more room and have less utility, owing to the politics of austerity.

Friedrich Nietzsche wrote in *The Will to Power* that "the higher man is distinguished from the lower man by his fearlessness and his readiness to challenge misfortune". It's a comment that doesn't quite sit in a Tory Manifesto but it could be rewritten and spun to show the power of any individual in a free market economy to strengthen themselves through adversity. In America it's called 'fail quick, fail often'.

I spent an afternoon at the 'Bright Buttons' pre-school in Cardiff and met with the workers there. It's hard not to be impressed by the work that a small organisation like this does and the valuable role it performs in the community. The pre-school has twenty children aged 1 - 4 and also takes in babies from 3 months upwards. It's Ofsted ranking was 'Good' at the last assessment and there is a waiting list to get in. I spoke with the Headteacher about children's life chances at this stage. She was very forthright and gave me a very direct opinion on the importance of a strong educational environment at an early age. Her view was that a child's life chances begin to be shaped as early as age 2, where the brain is undergoing enormous development. She was adamant that she could look at a child's parents and the way they interacted with the child and gain quick insights into the child's life chances. I was left wondering about my own parents and how they have effectively shaped me from birth, because all the research says that parenting is the number one thing. I also wondered at the causal association being made here and how this fed into wider Government agendas on early intervention such as those by the advisor Frank Field. Are children purely a product of their genetics and their upbringing? Can other things affect their life chances and how can we accommodate these? What about a good educational experience like these children are starting to get at Bright Buttons? There is evidence that a high quality early education environment can make a significant impact on children's life chances, so I was left a little disappointed that the Headteacher focused so much on the parents - did she not feel that herself and her staff were not making a difference in these children's lives? My conclusion is that early years learning can make a positive impact on children's life chances but of course it has to go hand in hand with nourishing parenting.

My attention was drawn by several people to the so called 'Fairness Premium' implicit in government thinking since 2010. In effect this is an instrument that attempts to target resources on a needs basis to children and their families. Boiled down to a simple statement it means resourcing children on an ongoing basis from early years according to need. In higher income families we see common attributes - family money, positive affirmation of schooling and reward for achievement. Under New Labour Sure Start centres were expressly set up as universal services to avoid the stigmatising impact of targeting services on those with the most need. Yet under the coalition of 2011 this became a focus of welfare austerity with a retrenchment back to the targeting of services. When I visited Bright Buttons, I was left with the inescapable reality that targeting also involves 'othering' processes. Other people's children are those identified as in need, people who are the focus of Government poverty and lifestyle agendas; yet the structural features of poverty are rarely blamed for the need for state intervention in family life. Individual families are deemed incapable of managing family life, making poor lifestyle choices and not giving their child the best of life chances. So is this about challenging the structural inequalities in society or just managing poverty?

A key question in all of this is one of liberty and intervention. Can, and more importantly, should, the state intervene and improve a child's life chances or for that matter a youth on the verge of a life of crime? Is this a role for the state or should it be the role of families? When do the scales tip in favour of needing some sort of state intervention in family life and how best should this be provided for fairness and equality to remain as a core value of a democratic society? The equation becomes more complicated, when we examine an array of outcomes based on inputs from childhood to adolescence. Just where in this unfolding set of circumstances can we make the most impact and who is responsible for it?

In my visit to St Helens in Merseyside, I went to a special school who work with children that have been regularly excluded from mainstream schools. I met with a group of six young people and their teacher. I discussed life chances with them and was surprised at their openness and candour. 'Will' described a situation of his father leaving when he was five. His mother began a series of unsuccessful relationships with different men and directed a huge amount of anger towards him in his childhood. He grew up imagining that this is how all families are. A series of meetings with a counsellor showed him that anger and violence in the home are not normal or in fact standard. The teacher described to me a common issue in young men forming relationships with women saying that in single parent households the lone parents' attitude to new relationships can have a profound effect on the child. 'Jamie' told me that he had been brought up by his Nan before she died. He spoke affectionately about her and said that when he was returned to his Mother's house, he encountered three half siblings who were being physically abused by his step father. The consequence for him was leaving home at the age of 15 and ending up in a church run refuge for children. He is now receiving counselling and support within a peer group at school. 'Warren' summarised the feelings of the group in talking about having a revised model of 'what normal looks like'. In essence this is being shown a way of being that is reciprocal, trusting and empathetic with those around you. My conclusion, is that there is no normal and systems often allow people to fall within the cracks.

Finally, in Bolton I met with a group of disabled adults, perhaps the most difficult in terms of evaluation of life chances from a neoliberal view point. Of course those with long term care needs can't be ushered into the workplace but they are valued members of society.

The group was in the process of making a video about their town with an inspired media worker 'Edgar'. He was quite clear that the life chances of disabled people should not be ignored. 'They're not here to be pushed around and maintained, they can be creative people and of course have viewpoints that are valuable,' he said. When I asked 'Lucy', one of the video-making participants, what the government should be doing she replied "Nothing without us".

My conclusion in following in the footsteps of IDJ, is that our country has to remain compassionate and understand differing needs and experiences. But what we see in the agenda of Ivan Dunhouse-Jones and his colleagues is that they have conflated life style with life chances, moving away from the original Weberian meaning. This is a huge political problem.

Some names have been changed to protect the individuals interviewed.

Pathways To Poverty
Family Breakdown
Educational Failure
Economic Dependency
Worklessness
Addiction
Personal Debt
CWL

Chapter 6

July

"Hottest Summer Since 1979"; "Cor, What A Scorcher"; "Freddie Starr Drank My Swimming Pool" **- the combination of a heatwave and the silly season is inspiring headline writers across the country. In London it's 29 degrees in the shade and a full meeting is underway at the Centre for Weasel Logic. On the agenda is the new report that they have just published - 'The Case For Cohesion and Clarity'. It is a comprehensive study of lucidity linkage in contemporary conurbations and the CWL staff are hoping it will be a major influence on the governments Life Chances Strategy.**

To enact their report, the CWL has embarked on a nationwide campaign to deliver 'Lucidity Champions' to every inner city area. The LC's, as they are known, send in blog reports with photos taken on mobile phones. This gives CWL a sense of connectedness to the communities that are facing the Pathways to Poverty struggles identified by Ivan Dunhouse-Jones.

In the room, are the board members and officers including Sir Stratham-Hyde, Chairman, Saskia Harkness, Acting CEO and Susannah Pringle, Campaigns Director. Secretary of State for Work and Pensions, Ivan Dunhouse-Jones, has sent his apologies. In the centre of the room is a large hand crafted boardroom table from Mozambique, a series of Peruvian recycled glass wine glasses are laid out formally along with bottles of Mersey Mineral Water.

The interior is minimalist, the only decoration a grouping of four framed photographs of Dunhouse-Jones meeting people on his tour, which has now become the heart of the IDJ myth – his Damascus moment leading to the setting up of the Centre for Weasel Logic. A striking image of a man wearing a high-vis jacket shows him standing alongside Dunhouse-Jones pointing at two large settees that have been torched in a back alley. Another image shows a woman with two children perched on her lap, with one the older child shouting directly at the camera.

"Susannah, I believe you have some important news for us on the report we published last week," says Sir Stratham-Hyde. Susannah is both excited and worried. She has some great news to share but Saskia is being a right bitch to her at the moment. Just because the news stories mention her by name and not Saskia.

"Yes, I do. We have had some excellent coverage in *The Telegraph*, the *Daily Saliva*. Even *The Image* were favourable, now isn't that something?" Susannah glows.

"Can you give us a brief run down on the detail?" Sir Stratham-Hyde asks.

"*The Telegraph* talks about the quality of our research and how it reflects our ability on the ground to gain a sense of what is going on in the North of England. Gradual decline of heavy industries and break down of the family unit, that kind of thing...The *Saliva* quotes us extensively as promoting the toughening up of government policies in relation to benefit scroungers – their words not mine of course – we usually say claimants...and *The Image* praises our ability to lobby for and influence policy change," she says.

"I think you'll find that the latter is in fact negative for us," says Saskia. "We want to distance ourselves from disparaging comments about 'think tanks' and lobbyists." Here it comes, thinks Susannah, Saskia's getting the knives out.

"At the Centre for Weasel Logic, we pride ourselves on our thoroughness, independence of thought and mastery of lucidity," Saskia, continues, as if reading from a crib-sheet.

"Anyway, well done, Susannah – a terrific effort and please thank your team for us," Sir Stratham-Hyde comments. Susannah smiles smugly at Saskia. One-nil to me, she thinks.

The room is hot and Susannah gets up to open a window. A car passes with music blaring out... 'Out on the wiley, windy moors, we'd roll and fall in green, you had a temper like my jealousy...'

Susannah returns to her seat around the table. "I love that track," she says. "My daughter is obsessed with Kate Bush."

"Thank you Susannah for that fascinating insight into your family life. Now I suggest we get back the the agenda," Saskia retorts. One all, thinks Susannah.

"Thank you Saskia. Can you give us a few pointers on where the research is heading in the run up to the election? I imagine we'll be aiming to lobby all political parties closely using our 'Weasel Bulletin' format that you've done so well with?" Sir Stratham-Hyde asks.

"Indeed, Sir, we will have two major insight studies coming out in September. One by Ian Wrath on 'Help for Homeless' and the other by Norma Cheadle called 'Social Housing Counts'."

"Forgive me, but these seem like topics that we might associate with Labour and the left traditionally?" Sir Straham-Hyde asks.

"Yes, I know. But we can reframe these issues as centre-right territory by emphasising the need to take a more proactive stance, helping individuals to become resilient, rather than a passive approach which simply encourages dependency. And the left, I might add, are rapidly fracturing into in-fighting groups and spending most of their time on twitter!" Saskia replies.

The room laughs. Susannah doodles 'Two-one to Saskia Smarm' on her meeting agenda and then scribbles it out.

An insight study for NASTY (National Association of Statutory Terminology) has shown that fractured leftist groups are spending up to 45% of their time fighting bitter Twitter wars with ever escalating hashtags. Examples include #shoutlouder, #shutitmoron and #travestyinred.

A series of photographs are passed around of Sir Stratham-Hyde visiting a council estate in Cardiff. They show him chatting with Somali refugees and representatives of the Somali Association of Great Britain.

"We'll put these on the homepage. They'll look great alongside the images of IDJ at St Paul's Carnival, tucking into goat curry," says Susannah.

"Let's move on to poverty," says Sir Stratham-Hyde.

"We hear rumours about problems with Universal Credit, but according to G4N, things are progressing well. The £200 million 'write off' is now confirmed. The digital by design seems to be working and early indicators are that people with good IT skills find the system a lot easier than the old one. We're assured that this time that people have got a grip."

Susannah thinks back to the time she briefly signed on after returning from Paraguay at the end of her gap year. Daddy said she didn't need to, but she wanted the experience. She rather enjoyed filling in the little 'looking for work' booklet and the bi-weekly chats with her job advisor. She even went on a CV writing workshop. The man running it was so sweet and she spent most of the session chatting to him about her work with orphan marmosets in San Pedro.

"And," Saskia continues, "we are signing off on our updated 'Pathways to Poverty' document to be sent to central government departments. The CWL will attribute poverty to family breakdown, educational failure, economic dependency, worklessness, addiction and personal debt."

"Thanks all," says Sir Stratham-Hyde and he heads off for lunch with his old chum Sir William B'astard, CEO of Precarity Disruption Consulting, a sub-contractor for Deep Hole via the Gravure 'Cloud as a Service' partnership.

Susannah, having been reminded about her previous charity work, eats her Pret a Manger avocado and herb salad wrap at her desk, looking at the '¡¡Oui Oui Ouistiti!!' website and tweeting cute pictures of miniature monkeys.

SHE, Shireen and Desiree are shown around the business development unit at Aspire Court. The managing agent shows them the lighting control, wi-fi and shared kitchen. The three women are happy that they have a space to develop Life Chances. The unit is about five metres square and painted mauve. The agent tells them that their set-up grant includes some basic IT training and laptops.

They decide to move in the desks that they have been given by Ubuntu, using a friends van. The following day the first group of co-workers arrive, who've heard about the project through Ubuntu and by word of mouth.

Desiree leads the session. She's new to jewellery making, but has been practising avidly and feels confident. Some of the women in the group have made jewellery before and people start swapping ideas and tips. Once the women are busy making they relax and start chatting about their lives. Desiree talks about her hopes and aims for the project and how they want to use the business as a campaigning hook. SHE joins in the conversation and talks about the governments Five Pathways to Poverty. She would like to work with the group to find a community centred alternative which moves away from the moral judgement that poverty is an individual lifestyle choice rather than a product of how society is structured. Desiree is slightly worried that they've gone in too hard with the politics, rather than concentrating on the making. But SHE is so fired up, Desiree couldn't have stopped her even if she had tried.

Hadi is due to make another representation to the immigration office. This means a long journey to Liverpool with Ayla, plus she'll miss a couple of days of school. Hadi has been through the 'Right to Remain' toolkit with Jonathan at Northside but she is not feeling that optimistic.

Following a phone call to the Liverpool Immigration Office, she is given a cancellation appointment at 10.15am on Wednesday 13th July. The journey from Cardiff to Liverpool by bus takes just over seven hours. Jonathan lends her £100 to cover the journey and an overnight place to stay. She doesn't like to take the money, but she has no option. She finds a cheap B&B in the Ropewalks area of Liverpool. Ayla is unsettled by the unfamiliar surroundings and it takes a long time to get her to sleep. They're woken up at 2am by the return of a Hen Party from a nearby club. The chaotic shouting and clicking of stiletto heels seems to go on for ages.

After eating a breakfast of peanut butter rolls Hadi brought along with her, they make their way to the Immigration Office and sit in the waiting area. As usual it is packed and the rising heat of the day makes it even more unbearable. At the entrance, people speaking various languages congregate, smoking and exchanging views.

Hadi has no lawyer and scant knowledge of the legal process. Jonathan has advised her to talk with other people who have sought the right to remain in the UK, although she finds this hard to do. She doesn't like talking about the reasons why she left Turkey. He has offered to be a McKenzie friend, a lay person who can support a litigant in court, but has only basic knowledge of the legal frameworks surrounding asylum cases like hers. He isn't qualified so although he can give some support it's not the same as having a lawyer who knows all the ins and outs of the law. The whole thing is so complicated and things keep changing.

She has found the lack of choice about where she can live extremely hard, having been moved around various forms of housing. But this is still better than the uncertainty back home in Turkey.

Her name is called and she enters the interview room. After the now familiar opening statements by the interviewer, she is asked if she has any additional supporting evidence. She produces a large A4 folder full of documents and passes several pieces of paper to the interviewer. He examines them.

Hadi looks down at the brown carpet in the interview room, Ayla sits quietly reading a book she has brought along with her from school. The evidence Hadi has supplied consists of threatening emails written in Turkish. She has supplied crude translations from her own knowledge of English.

"I will place these on file so that we can decide if any of the grounds for giving you leave to remain in the UK would apply. I have to tell you that falsification of any evidence supplied is a criminal offence and can lead to deportation. I am obliged to have these inspected by a qualified language expert for authentication."

"I can see that you are applying for a fee waiver for yourself and your child. In your case this is likely to be successful as you have no resources, I can see that from the file…" he says baldly. Hadi feels extremely uncomfortable with a stranger laying bare her life before her.

"I am noting your academic achievements and I will take copies of the certificates, again these will need to be verified. I can see you are actually, well educated…" he tails off and then proceeds to sign a piece of paper in front of him.

"I now have to ask you if you have anything more to say by way of evidence at this representation stage?"

"I want to say that if I have to go back, I will be persecuted and my family will be in danger," she says.

The interview concludes in just over twenty minutes. She leaves the building and walks out with Ayla into a hot sunny day, and they make their way on foot to the bus station to wait for the coach back home.

Asha is cooking at home in Bristol, preparing okra and vegetable soup, Abdi's favourite. At 3pm, she walks to the junior school to collect the children, and then onto the secondary school to pick up her two eldest. She knows many of the children at secondary school walk home by themselves, but she needs to know her children are safe.

Abdi is out working extra hours for the bus company, Fast Fleet. Asha is now very worried about their financial situation, as the Universal Credit has been cut dramatically from last month. She paid the council tax and the water bill but now they are down to the last few pounds in her purse. Abdi doesn't understand the system and asks her to find out what's going on.

The children watch TV and she takes the chance to phone the G4N Universal Credit support line. She sits in a queue for over 20 minutes.

"…You are…number 10…in the queue…please hold…we are receiving a high volume of calls..." The system whirrs round with the occasional blast of a Bach Fugue in C Minor.

"Hello, you're through to Celine, what is your name and how can I help? Please note that calls may be recorded for training purposes only."

"Yes, my name is Asha Silano, and my…our benefit has been cut, can you explain why?" Asha asks politely.

She is taken through the various security questions and the call handler asks her to wait while she finds the case. In the background at the call centre there is near panic as the main back up system is not functioning. This means that the call handlers cannot see 'live' data anymore. They have been briefed to print out data from another back up.

Asha waits for nearly 10 minutes, becoming increasingly worried about the cost of the call.

"Hello, sorry to keep you waiting Asha, we're experiencing a few technical difficulties here at the moment. Let me see, ahh, I think I have it – how much was your husband paid last month?" she asks.

"I think he did usual amount around 35 hours, I don't think he did any overtime last month, so it should be the same as usual."

"Ok, thank you. The Universal Credit system is set up with real time information. We receive data on your husband's earnings from HMRC and they receive it from his employer. I can see here that he did in fact earn more than usual in June, so your payment will reflect that."

Asha finds the system complicated and struggles to understand the Universal Credit 'taper' and 'real time information' system.

"But I am sure my husband did not do overtime in June," Asha says.

"Let me just calculate this. It looks like he did 52 hours. Your husband worked more, so he gets less benefit and we do that more quickly now. It protects everyone from over or under payments, you see…" Celine says, "is there anything else I can help you with?"

"No, no thank you," Asha says and the call ends. She wants to ask more but is is worried about the cost of the call.

When Abdi returns she tells him about the call. He is unhappy and they argue about the fact that they have no money. She doesn't understand why they have received less Universal Credit this month. She asks him to talk to the office when he goes in to work, although the finance administrator has never been very helpful.

The following day he discovers that the pay roll department had submitted the wrong number of hours, mixing up his records with another bus driver who had done overtime in June.

Debra has invited Secnach to the professional development programme she has set up, which she has called 'Insights'. Debra has no budget to bring anyone in and she has relied on favours to keep the scheme going. The social workers enjoy it, as it is the only social space they have during work time that gives them the opportunity to talk about anything but their caseloads.

In the meeting room, Secnach is talking to the group.

"Zantonica looks like a paradise from the outside. It has long beaches, sun throughout the year and coconut trees. But the people do have problems similar to the problems people have in the UK," Secnach clicks through a series of slides as she talks.

The next slide is of Secnach and her friend under the Dragon Blood Tree. The trees have an umbrella shape creating shade beneath a deeply dense network of interwoven branches.

Secnach shows a picture of her family home. The building sits with many others up high on a rock face. The white designs of the windows suggest Moorish architecture and, from a distance, the buildings resemble a Bruegel painting.

"I have a younger sister, she is called Yintra," she says.

A picture of a girl appears on the screen. She is about 14 years old, has long dangling ear-rings and a bright red jacket. She squints at the camera in a half smile.

“Most people think Zantonica looks like a Utopia, so why would we need a welfare system, when the place looks so rich?” says Secnach.

“But culture and the economy are under pressure. There have been changes due to tourism and ecological problems too. So, my job is to work with families and young people to try to shape this. What we are trying to do is to form an identity that relates to our culture and environment. We want to respond to the changes, like new technology and education, in such a way that we can have our version of these things, not just an imported lifestyle from America or Europe.”

“It does look very beautiful,” says Debra.

“Yes, but the beauty of our land is partly maintained by policy. No large hotels are allowed to be built on Zantonica, no tourist complexes with English pubs or American burger bars. When people visit from abroad they must live like Zantonicans, stay in the same kind of dwellings we live in, and eat in the restaurants we eat at and buy food from the same markets. Visitors are embraced and invited into our culture but they must also respect it.”

Secnach flicks through some more slides showing the distinctive Zantonican housing and fresh fruit and vegetables at a market.

“We work with teachers and families and the children all together in sessions and we talk about all of the environmental concerns that people have. We always do our work in groups, always.”

“Looks amazing,” says Sharon, the team manager, “but what about marriages and that kind of thing?”

“The family set-up in Zantonica is matriarchal. It is the woman who proposes to the man, and family wealth is handed down through the female line. Family names are similar to those in Iceland. If you are a girl, you use your mother's first name with the letter E as a prefix. My mother's name is Fil, so my last name is E’fil. If I were a boy my name would be N’kom – my fathers name is Kom and boys have the prefix N.”

“The family wealth handed down the female line, I like the sound of that,” jokes Sharon.

"The main problem we face is trying not to live in the past and just be the subject of tourism. The funny thing is, the only people from the West who come here to live are the super-rich. They are the biggest danger to our way of life."

"Is that because of the speed boats?" asks Debra.

Diane is sitting in a restaurant near the O2 in Greenwich. The conference she has just attended on 'New Journalism' was filled with dull presentations from star journalists pontificating about their importance and unique talents. Time for some real work. She gets down to finishing off the central article of the series, looking at work:

Make Work Pay – The Future of Work

Looking for an opening quote for this article, I was struggling to find something that fits. I kept coming across pieces like 'Addicted to Success' written by ripped 30-something men with titanium white teeth, proselytising about their magic breakthroughs.

I found myself wondering - is there something special about IDJ and is he now the guru of poverty? This thought left me disturbed. I can't pinpoint why but it is something to do with the moral assumptions and high manner of authority in him.

In our time, a new 'chancer' culture of online gurus has emerged. They all seem the same in one respect - they know what the future will look like. Maybe because they have convinced themselves that they are in some perceived future of their own making and the rest of us are left behind in some Neanderthal dung heap waiting to be dug up by the University of the Future's Archaeology Department.

Readers may have come across the work of Ernst Negri, whose recent book 'Small is the new BIG' has caused a stir in the political world. Negri's argument is that the narrow planning for welfare in the digital age is still connected to short-term political goals in European countries. He sees the potential of Universal Credit in the UK, but for very different reasons to those intended by IDJ. Negri sees a near future in which artificial intelligence will replace many of the low paid jobs associated with what are called 'the working poor'. In an earlier article, I mentioned the picking factories at online grocer Vocado and the phenomenal advances made in their business. The super-giant corporation Nile has a business plan that is aiming to supply anything the same day it is ordered, with complete automation. That means no humans at all. Yes, really.

Negri believes that large scale platforms such as UC are a necessary evil of the technology revolution. This, he says, will open the doors to unconditional credit (or what he calls basic income guarantee). Basic income guarantee would give everyone in the country, irrespective of status, a minimum amount of money.

He argues that UC will pave the way to BIG, particularly alongside the rise in personal tax allowance threshold and ideas about aligning tax and national insurance. We might see a transformation of the tax system where everyone receives a given amount and the present tax thresholds would be abolished.

Our future life chances may not be built upon work but leisure and play. So, if BIG happens, it will be because there is no work, but you will be given money to live and time to do other things – but will it be enough money to do things, or just to survive?

Just imagine, logging on to your personal life chances account and selecting options for spending your time each day. The food arrives from Vocado in the morning, the house is fully automated from your mobile phone and a driverless car awaits to whisk you away to your pilates class. Of course the pilates class could be streamed into your home via real time screens cleverly curved over the patio windows. Or you might want to see some real people this week, for a change? But, we know that these utopian pictures are more akin to 1950s adverts for ideal lives, than actual circumstances.

Negri imagines health care and online aggregation of choices to be able to advise people on their lifestyle choices, aided by personal gadgets. Of course we already see the power of search engines in aggregating real time data to the NHS and others. Negri is telling us that this automation of lifestyle is with us and we need to put into place the social and political frameworks to deal with it.

A further and darker point that Negri makes is that advances in the development of algorithms and sense and sensor data from a variety of points will enable accurate prediction of individual life chances. Imagine being told when you will die?

The issue at stake here is the conflict between the state and the individual. Will we see general practitioners performing life chances assessments online with the populace at large? Will people be refused care if they don't cooperate? Could the NHS become a vast big data repository with its own ethical stance on how we live our lives? Are the elite politicians about to become the ultra-stick waving life marshals of the future? Can I hear you say this is already happening or is there more to be done?

I am still disturbed at self-appointed gurus such as IDJ and I am alarmed by Negri's insights. It seems that the general populace is unaware of the massive shifts in society. It will become necessary to use technology to reduce costs and encourage more awareness of risk, but we seem a million miles from understanding this momentous shift from the welfare state to one of technological monitoring.

On the matter of basic income guarantee, it seems that across the spectrum of political opinion this may become a reality, even if it is against the grain of neo-liberal thought.

Of course it is a matter of thinking more widely about where the scant resources are placed to bring more people into the debate in an informed way.

Chapter 7

August

Toby sits with Charlie in the middle of his open plan loft apartment in London Bridge, sucking on some beers and messing about with the bits of tech that litter his floor. Charlie works for Anderson and Johns, a top law firm dealing with intellectual property, and someone Toby taps for advice, both personal and work related. Toby and Charlie first met at Cosplay Mania, a costume and role-play convention Charlie's then girlfriend had organised.

Toby and Charlie shared a love of *Star Wars* (Toby had put his religion as 'Jedi Knight' on the 2011 census), and though neither of them went as far as dressing up, they were more than ok with their girlfriends indulging. As Toby said, if his girlfriend Suzie wanted to dress as Princess Leia in *The Return of the Jedi* (gold bikini and all), who was he to stop her? Charlie's girlfriend had left him for some Boba Fett look-a-like and Toby's girlfriend had swapped Cosplay for the ukelele. But they still liked to hang out every now and then.

Toby sparks up a spliff and shows Charlie a shell command to hack into his iPhone.

"Pretty simple warez really, once you've created a fake token. I can access your banking passwords, your email, Facebook. If you've done it online, I can see it online," Toby boasts, exhaling slowly and passing the spliff to Charlie.

It's Saturday but Toby can still feel the pressure from work in his head. While he feigns an outwardly relaxed attitude, inside he knows that things are not going well – particularly since Jem 'the enforcer' appeared on the scene. Deep Hole was one major kludge and whilst he was adept at dodging crapplets, he might just end up #outonhisarse through no fault of his own.

He decides to sound out Charlie on the current status of Deep Hole. "Sure, tell me the story, Chatham House rules and all that," says Charlie.

"Well man, I have this real fucking dilemma. On the one hand I've been asked to fix this system and work the firm out of a hole but on the other hand I'm feeling more and more uncomfortable with what's going on here. I mean, we all bend the rules don't we? But ever since this Jem dude from the ministry has moved into the frame, the pressure has been mounting. So, last week, he was right in my face giving me the full heat of the deal. So, I said to him that we can get the thing up and running but it needs more time and if we go to full roll out too soon, then we risk opening ourselves up to major issues. Basically, the general punters engaging with a half-baked solution," Toby says.

Charlie takes a long drag on the spliff and winces his reply through the smoke.

"It's pretty simple Toby, you have to do what's right, not confuse yourself or have misplaced loyalty. Put something on the record, as part of an audit trail, just an email will do. Tell your boss what the real situation is and protect yourself man, because when these things open up in the press or even at committee, you could be roasted. So, send your boss a note and take the pressure off."

"I've done that already, I've sent Barry more emails than I can remember saying the thing won't work and we need staged roll out, but every time he comes back and says jog it along. So, that's what I'm trying to do...and it's eating me up, man. It's like I've started to grow carbuncle on my neck like Richard E Grant in 'How to Get Ahead in Advertising'. Only my pimple has a fucking social conscience." Toby moans.

"Wow, Toby, bro! Full kudos to your fledgling moral pustule!" Charlie laughs, the hot ash from the spliff sizzling as he taps it into his half empty beer bottle. "I know you, you like to storm and fix – and it's a part of who you are – but there are situations where you just can't do that."

"But, Charlie, this is fucking serious, if I don't fix it they will torch me. And if I do a rush job the system will torch fucking loads of people who have already been well and truly fucked by the fucking state!"

Charlie hands the smouldering roach back to Toby. "We had this case the other day. A dispute about OLED screens between two companies. This small start-up company was insistent that they had invented the X widget but the big multinational company said that X widget was part of a contract including intellectual property. We had to tell the start-up to walk away because they couldn't go against the multinational and the powerful litigators they had behind them."

"So, are you telling me to walk?" says Toby.

"I'm telling you that down the line you may have to walk, talk or build a strong case internally that defends you. Deffo," says Charlie.

Charlie gets a call from his new girlfriend, Ophelia. Toby stubs out the spliff and taps something into his laptop.

"I've got to go, man, Ophelia wants to meet up at Austerity," says Charlie.

"Where's that?" says Toby.

"It's over near Shepherd's Bush, they do a killer sea bass."

Life Chances has some rather predictable local press coverage. *The Bristol Echo* sent round a journalist with a camera to snap SHE, Shireen and Desiree wearing some of their jewellery designs, and to do a short interview. The subsequent piece is given the headline "Single Mums take a Life Chance". As SHE points out to the others, she's not actually a single mum. *The Bristol Echo* never represents people of colour honestly. But at least the piece managed to get over the political side of their project. Give with one hand and take with the other. And it has gotten them some interest on social media, with 134 new followers on Twitter and a lot of Facebook likes.

They decide to keep the working team set at 10 people for the time being. Over the first six weeks they have managed to develop a range of designs based on a simple circular logo that reflects the solidarity they are trying to fuse into their project.

Shireen walks down Stapleton Road towards the Life Chances unit. People are hanging out on the street as temperatures reach 32 degrees. Cars pass her with sub bass resonating out and bouncing off the walls of the surrounding buildings. A dog laps water furiously out of a bowl outside one of the shops. She can't wait to see everyone and tell them the news. She gives a little skip as she approaches the unit.

"Sorry I'm late but I have some really big news," Shireen gets herself a drink of water and sits down at the making table.

"I've been contacted by a social enterprise investment fund, EcoEth, that wants to put some money into Life Chances. What they do is give money to communities like ours to support activities that create more cohesion and jobs. They just want to give us the money up front and they don't want any acknowledgment at all!"

Desiree is sceptical. "Well, me nuh trust it cos tings jus don't happen like that, there must be a catch in it, nobody gives you something for nothin. Look how sister Bryant get child credit fund and they were mad to take her to court and crape de money back from her. De poor woman was so distressed she ad to call her pastor fe pray for deliverance. So mi nuh trus dem; the devil is a liar."

Shireen feels a bit deflated. She was imagining that everyone would be over the moon but Desiree and a few others are just sitting there looking suspicious. SHE, unusually, has not said a word. Shireen tries to give more detail.

"The social investor fund is supported by philanthropists from all over the world. They all put in a certain amount of money and then they look for projects that can make a difference. They've funded something up in Knowle West already, it's all legal you know," Shireen tries to sound more forthright.

"Me ah go pray it. It does sound good mi hafta admit. And me see you're excited. But look here Shireen, we mus be careful who's money we tek you know, we nuh want nobody to call us fraud. So look into it further." Desiree, playing it safe again, thinks Shireen. Why is no-one as excited as her about the offer of funding?

"Me going to the revival meeting at church and also we have to meet de journalist Diane. She says she's going to write something about us." Desiree looks at her watch. "SHE gave her a good interrogation over the phone yesterday, so she knows not to mess, plus we've met her a few times now, and I think we can trust her to do something better than *The Bristol Echo* piece." The women round the table shake their heads and laugh.

As if on cue, Diane pops her head round the doorway. "Room for one more?" she asks. The women stop talking and busy themselves with the jewellery. Shireen feels frustrated not to talk more, but like the other women, she doesn't want to discuss money in front of a stranger. SHE introduces Diane to the group and offers her a chair round the table.

"I'll just sit here in the corner and watch and see how you work if that's ok?" says Diane.

"No, it nuh gwan suh you have to be part of the circle," Desiree indicates a free chair and hands her a pair of pliers.

The group begin making jewellery and a production line is evident.

Each item is placed in a presentation box with the Life Chances logo on it. Inside is a message to the person purchasing it. Shireen shows Diane a sample message written by one of the group members.

"We are not just selling jewellery, we're sharing positivity," Shireen reads out. "So each message sends out that hope to another person. We as a people in our community, the ones who are being ground down by the system, persecuted and devalued, need hope."

Diane puts aside her journalistic cynicism and lets herself feel the general energy in the room. She can see a female solidarity but one that is comprised of people who do not fit with the co-operative movement resurgence that she's seen across the country. There's nothing trendy about this. No tattoo sleeves or ear plug ear-rings. No burlesque styling or dip dyed hairdos.

Diane starts to bend some copper wire with her pliers and tunes into a discussion going on about children and school over the other side of the table. She finds herself actually enjoying the making, even though her necklace looks decidedly lopsided.

SHE, Shireen and Desiree move over to the other side of the unit and start sorting out teas and coffees for everyone, taking the opportunity to quietly discuss the offer of social enterprise money.

"What I can't understand is how they just give it to us, no questions asked," Desiree says.

"They have been watching us for a while, they've spoken to the housing association and they've also met with people who have bought stuff from us. They've built up a picture of us and they like what they see. So, it's simple."

"Exactly," says SHE. Shireen is glad SHE is starting to engage in the conversation.

"But where does the money actually come from?" asks Desiree.

"The person that phoned me said it's an ethical investment fund but it's not an investment for shares, it's an investment in us..." Shireen tails off because she still finds it unbelievable too.

"So, how much money are they actually offering us?" asks SHE, getting down to the nitty-gritty. Shireen pauses and a half smile, half grimace crosses her face.

"£185,000," Shireen says. SHE exhales loudly.

Desiree is shocked. She can't believe it. But she has been praying to God for a miracle, to change how her life is going. Maybe that's the miracle.

"Together we need to decide what to do with dat kinda skrilla," SHE looks at the women working away round the table.

"I don't know, SHE, but imagine, we could get the other unit and maybe bring in some more people, start another group," Shireen starts pouring milk into the teas and coffees.

"We need to do our research on who runs this and what their background is. Let's find out how other projects they have funded have done. Maybe Diane can help us," says SHE, nodding her head and pouting her lips towards Diane, "You can make yourself useful."

They break for lunch and SHE, Desiree, Shireen and Diane sit on a wall outside the unit talking. Diane is really impressed by what she's seen. She admits to the women that she was cynical about their project, as to what it could achieve, but she thinks they maybe on to something. She asks them about their plans for the future.

Before they can answer, Diane's phone interrupts the conversation. 'Caller ID hidden' flashes up on the screen. "Excuse me, I'd better take this," Diane says and walks over to the car park.

"Yo. This is the bloke you met a few months ago in the bar at the Bristol Hotel. I've been following your articles in *The Image*. Impressive stuff and spot on, double plus plus." It's Toby. Diane recognises the nasal estuarine accent and slightly silly way of talking.

"Oh, you, yes I remember, I didn't expect to hear from you again," Diane answers.

"Yeah, well I said a bit too much without realising who you are. Thanks to your articles I've had to keep my head down big stylee. I'm asking you, nicely, to lay off the Bristol angle, or...bada boom bada bing, if you get my meaning." Toby tries to sound menacing but fails.

Diane has to stop herself from giggling. Who did he think he was, Tony Soprano?

"I'm not going to stop writing about Deep Hole, Toby. In fact I'm going to write about it again in the next piece. It's a public interest story and I've witnessed the PR control your people have over everything. Your boss gave me nothing when I interviewed him and the spin agency stonewalled me out of the building!"

"That's not what I'm saying. I want to give you the real story on Deep Hole, go totally wikileaks, but it needs to be done in a way that I stay anonymous, you get me?"

Diane's mind whirrs. Toby has the social aplomb of a spanner, but he is in the right place to deliver what he is promising.

"Well I can't absolutely guarantee anonymity, but I'll do my best." Diane replies. She doubts that she's got another Edward Snowden on the end of the line, but then what if she has?

Toby can't quite believe it, is he really going to blow the lid off? He is pretty sure he can tell his tale without framing himself. And even if it does come out, there are large swathes of the hacker community who would fete him as a hero for whistle-blowing. That might be even better. That thought spurs him on.

"Deep Hole doesn't really work…we've been trying to get it up and running for three years…but it's not going to work probably for another three years…they brought us in to try and tidy things up but we've found a total mess…manual input of data…lost data…security holes in the software…cost over-runs…invoicing chaos…sign offs for work that appears not to have happened…people left hanging for weeks on end with nothing to live on."

"So why are you telling me this if you're trying to gag me?" Diane says.

"I'm telling you this because I am under major pressure to bring it all home, safe, sound and operational and it can't be done. Not a chance… So I'm asking you for some help. Give me a bit of time to square things my end and I'll give you the full story," Toby says.

Diane fumbles for a notebook and pen in her bag. "Ok, let's be careful here," she says, now serious in tone.

"I am being careful, this is an encrypted phone. What I'm telling you could be attributed to a number of people at G4N. If they find out it's me they will probably give me a concrete jacket and lob me in the river."

"No, they won't do that," says Diane. She smirks, he really does seem to think this is some sort of geek mafia movie.

"I will give you a full interview but you'll have to agree to cover it anonymously, would you do that?" asks Toby, "and I need some time before it all comes out, and I want to tell it my way."

"I can't make any promises in how or if I will write your story, but I will keep you anonymous," says Diane.

"Well, ok, yeah. Whatevs. I'll phone you again. Laters," Toby says and cuts the call dead feeling a sense of dread mixed in with the kind of adrenaline buzz he hasn't felt since he bungee jumped off a bridge in Kuala Lumpur.

Diane finishes her notes and walks back to the three women who are still talking.

"Everything ok?" asks Desiree.

"Oh, yes, just someone who thinks he has a story. I get these kind of calls all the time."

Jem and Barry meet over at the Ministry. The period of time to resolve the system is now drawing to a close. Barry knows that the meeting will be tough.

"Ok, Barry is it all fixed with Deep Hole? Or are we going to be on the rocks with IDJ on this one?" Jem asks.

"Mostly. We are approaching an overview of pressure points and the full reset plan is now complete, on paper that is, not practically," Barry deliberately obfuscates the matter.

"Barry, don't give me the run around on this, I need you to be fully up front with me so that I can go to IDJ with a clear story. He wants it all to be fully transparent. We've spent the last three years in an IT procurement hall of mirrors and nothing less than full disclosure on our position will do, you understand this don't you Barry?"

Barry smiles through gritted teeth. "I do understand this, Jem. And with the greatest respect, we are trying our very best to do what you've asked us to do. We've done a full reset and we've abandoned agile completely. We are back on the 'waterfall' method."

"Waterfall, that was never a good term was it Barry? In Britain we've wasted hundreds of millions on IT waterfalls. We could have built 15 hospitals, 20 Olympic Stadiums and given away painkillers in the street to those needing them. Right now all I need to know is how long this is going to take." Jem sighs, thinking about the bollocking he's going to get from IDJ.

"I need another two weeks," says Barry.

At his office at the Ministry of Work and Pensions, Ivan Dunhouse-Jones is having a meeting with his private secretary Bernard. A discussion ensues about the rollout of Community Lucidity Champions and the importance of them in rebuilding the family.

"You don't think this looks a bit like China, you know a woman on every street listening and reporting up the chain to the party?" says IDJ.

"No, the Lucidity Champions are going down really well with everyone and a great idea of yours too," says the secretary.

"Oh I'm not taking the credit for that, but my people over at the CWL can," IDJ demurs.

"We have hit a slight snag, sir, with 16th of August as a date for the press junket with some tame LC's, as we've started calling the Lucidity Champions," Bernard smirks. "You've got a meeting booked with Jem on the Deep Hole update and there's no way you can be in two places at once,"

"We'd better put Jem back then hadn't we," says IDJ.

"Yes, sir, we'd better put him back a fortnight…" the secretary agrees.

"Is that all now Bernard? I've got a 10 o'clock with Jeffers and then an 11.15 with that woman MP from Sheffield and her ideas on reviving the local economy by turning the closed down steel factories into tourist destinations. God forbid."

Bernard raises one eyebrow "Yes of course sir." He gives a slight nod of his head and then turns and exits the room. At his computer he flicks through his contact database and dials a number.

"I have some good news for you, Jem, IDJ can't see you this week, he wants to put it back a fortnight. I imagine that will give your people a bit of a breather?" Bernard smiles down the receiver.

"Thanks Bernard, helpful as ever," Jem says hanging up. God he hated that thin-lipped little grammar school boy. Bernard, Jem thought, had watched too many episodes of *Yes, Minister*'

Diane spends the next week following IDJ's footsteps across the country, getting the train from Newcastle to Glasgow. She then hires a car and drives east towards Easterhouse on the Lochend Road. On the left are new brick built family homes, on the right are remnants of the old estate with security cameras patrolling the area. The split is almost like a time rift with the 2000s on one side and the 1960s on the other.

A bare chested man looks across at her, his body pale white but muscular. He has a mobile phone clamped to his head and slashed jeans. His designer boxer shorts peek out over a shirt tied around his waist. He struts confidently to wherever he is going.

She passes a single storey pub covered in graffiti with a blackened frontage. The windows are tinned up. An Indian restaurant with red frontage has its shutters pulled down. A line of women and children queue at an ice cream van, chatting in the sunshine. On the blind side of the ice cream van, as she passes, is a crudely painted picture drawn from the animated film *Cars*. The continuing presence of CCTV cameras on tall masts reminds her of Belfast and parts of Bristol she has visited. In contrast there is a lushness to the ash trees planted alongside the road. At the end of Lochend Road there is a small wind turbine whirring around slowly against the striated sky.

She stops in an area that could be described in estate agent speak as 'awaiting regeneration'. Patches of scrubland are dotted with signs of fires and dumped mattresses and children playing football with half-inflated balls. One of the children shouts at her in the car as she stops and flicks a middle finger at her. She gets out of her hire car and starts walking across a partly turfed area, ineffectually ring fenced by security fencing trampled on and scattered aimlessly. It seems ironic to her that words like 'Loch' capture the magical beauty and wonder of Scotland but here just off Lochend Road, it is literally the end of the line.

"This place is fucked!" she hears behind her. She turns startled to see an elderly man with an overweight Jack Russell huffing at his side. The man walks towards her and points to a burned out building. The dog obediently stops when he does. "I remember when this was row on row of tenement housing, to house the workers at the textile factories, ye ken?"

The man looks around him and then back at Diane.

"You're not from round here are you lassie. Are ye lost? What have ye come here fir?" the man says in a thick Glaswegian accent.

"I'm a journalist and I'm writing about places like this around the country." Diane looks around at the decay and desolation surrounding her.

"Aye, ye cud set a filam aboot Beirut here couldn't ye?" the man says.

"Do you mind if I ask you some questions?" counters Diane. "You obviously know this area and its history?"

"Aye, aye, I do. Ask away. I've nowt better to do," he replies, taking a treat from his pocket and giving it to the dog.

"My name is Diane Butler, I'm a freelance journalist. I'm writing about life chances and Ivan Dunhouse-Jones. I'm following the journey he took in 2009 around deprived areas in the UK, for a series of articles in *The Image*."

"Oh aye. I've read your articles down the library. And I'll tell you this, will'nah get much for yer money around here though, mentioning that man's name! And am not sure folk will take too kindly to being called deprived, I'll tell ye that. People round here still have their pride, ken?"

"Yes, I'm sorry. I guess I'm using the terminology that Dunhouse-Jones used," Diane apologies. "Can I ask you your name and how old you are?" says Diane.

"I'm Duncan McMasters and I am 71," he replies directly.

Diane is surprised and pleased that Duncan has read her articles in *The Image*. He explains that the area is due for regeneration but the money has run out and that generally the economy is struggling.

She spends over an hour walking and talking with Duncan, who turns out to be an ex-railway worker. Duncan tells her about the New Labour period of regeneration with large swathes of the old estate coming down and new buildings being put up in their place. He describes the drug gangs that ruled over the estate for long periods and how three generations of people have grown up without real jobs. He expresses the anger and despair brought about by the change of government and the apparent inevitability of Scottish independence, as the Tories continue with punitive benefit cuts while singing the tune of One Nation Conservatism.

"How exactly can this happen in the modern world?" Duncan asks. "If you are set on using Dunhouse-Jones's bullshit words, then this is the most deprived area of Western Europe, right here! The people are being punished day in, day out."

Diane feels that Duncan is interviewing her and she doesn't have any answers. She wonders if her presence feels prurient to Duncan.

"Nay, we need more people like yersel coming up here and telling our story. The truth is that the folk of Easterhouse have drifted from new homes under New Labour to the insecurity you talk about in your articles," Duncan says. "Now if they do find jobs they don't pay enough or provide enough security to raise a family. Mr Dunhouse-Jones wants them all to be in work and raise families doesn't he? That won't happen without job security."

Diane listens intently and agrees that job security is a key question in life chances. She wonders if making work pay is the same as making life work. Probably not.

"The old jobs of my generation were jobs fer life," Duncan says. "Now ye'd be lucky to have a zero hours contract for fifteen days!"

Diane thanks Duncan for his time and he wishes her good luck in her writing. He directs her to a nearby shopping precinct.

"Everything is called Phoenix here," he says with dark humour.

"Phoenix Shopping Arcade, Phoenix Housing, Phoenix Bank, Phoenix ice cream, and even Phoenix bog roll!"

He strolls away with his dog across the scrubland and past the mangled security fencing.

Diane walks around the area taking photos on her phone. She comes across a ground floor flat with a bed of flowering pansies and a small well-manicured lawn. There are concrete patio stones and an array of pots with flowers planted neatly. In the flat above several improvised washing lines dry an array of children's clothes. The roof has been remade on top of the tenement, along with air extraction vents.

She walks back to the hire car and starts writing the next article in free hand in her note book.

Jonathan, the Dragon 360 community worker, sits at his desk in the open plan office at Northside in Cardiff. There is a cheery atmosphere in the room and the tea round arrives with biscuits. The Dragon 360 programme has received additional funding from the Welsh government, and Jonathan is feeling excited. He has been invited to present the pilot work they have done in the Northside area. He ploughs through hundreds of images that he has taken of sessions working with local people. He selects two of the women that they have worked with over the last two months. He knows that the breakthroughs are precarious but feels strongly that their stories and progress need to be told.

He completes his preparation and walks over to the Welsh Assembly building on the Harbourside of the city to give his presentation.

"Client 'N' has been through the 360 work with us at Northside. She is a doctor and has one child. She left North Africa with only two suitcases and her daughter, fleeing the violence there. Consulting with 'N', we identified three people to work on a '360 Life Plan' with her. The first thing they did was to look at her health and that of her child. At this stage she needed culturally specific counselling support and to connect with trusted people. Both her and her child needed to begin the process of grounding themselves in Cardiff and they needed reassurance that their housing and basic needs could be stabilised. We have done this now. Then we needed to look at schooling and how that was going and we found that the child had adapted well to the new environment and was doing better than the mother. We have realised that the children can often be a way in for the adults, as school and the culture of school can help children understand where they are. Because, if you have come from North Africa to Cardiff, there are differences!" Jonathan says.

The audience, who have been listening intently, share a laugh. Among them are Assembly Members, councillors, social workers and representatives from other non-government organisations across the city. Jonathan shows a slide that he has created of 'N's' journey. It is a revealing way to show the obstacles that N has faced. A second slide shows a timeline of activities associated with N's time in the UK.

"What we found is that N had been travelling all over the UK to various agencies and attempting to make sense of the complexity of our regulatory systems, in particular the bureaucratic systems around her being able to practice medicine in this country. The Jobcentre was of absolutely no use to N – they could not a) provide the specialised advice and support she needed to find work as a doctor and b) they had no training themselves in working with people from a wide range of cultural backgrounds.

They had no sense of what it is like to try and make a new life in a completely different culture, having fled a violent and life threatening situation, without a support structure of friends or family. Dragon 360, as well as providing counselling support is working with N to improve her English. It will then fund the medical and language qualifications she needs to gain in order to work as a doctor."

The delegates seem impressed by Jonathan's presentation.

"We have now located a local GP who is mentoring N over the next three months. She will work with the three of us to assist her in the process of getting back into work. Once she has found a position as a GP she has agreed to work a minimum of three years in that role. Of course N has been able to keep her benefits while she is going through 360. Without that she couldn't possibly do any of it. We have submitted a preliminary report to the university people who are carrying out the study and they are writing this up.

One of the things they have done is to bring in a social economist and she is doing a social return on investment analysis of N's case. What they are hoping to do is to show that over a three to five year term the investment in terms of support for N actually costs less than her moving around state agencies in search of solutions and relying on benefits. The cost factor at the front end to pay us professionals is of course included in those equations."

Jonathan receives a round of applause and takes questions from the floor.

"What are the key barriers you find in your pilot Dragon 360 cases?" asks a woman in the front row.

"The main one is immigration status. We have to use different channels based on people's ability to work in the UK. N had British citizenship so we could move fast with her. Another client, H, did not, so we've had to work with her in a less intensive way. However, we have been advised that Dragon 360 is for anyone in the UK regardless of their immigration status," says Jonathan.

"But surely the resources need to be targeted at Welsh people?" asks another person.

"The directive from the Welsh Assembly is quite clear. Dragon 360 is about confronting the chaos that people face across the board as a result of the crisis all over the world. So we are working with people who are long term residents of the city, those who have come recently and some who have been sent here from other UK cities."

"But surely we won't have the resources to scale this up beyond a pilot will we?"

"The university study is critical in that respect. What we will begin to see is peoples' life chances plotted against their choices and the cost of maintaining them in the country over often prolonged periods while they establish their immigration status. We don't have those figures at the moment, but we have some early indicators. If you look at it in the near-term then it is expensive, but if you look at it over three to five years then it looks like it pays off."

"Won't this kind of thing act as a magnet to other immigrants to come here, when our resources are already stretched?" suggests a local councillor.

"The answer is in the question," says Jonathan. "We actually need big government to look at public resources across the board because we aren't coping as it is. We don't have any more suitable social or private housing, for example. We need new ideas that are sensitive to real people. So we need to carry on working with the kinds of people who will use Dragon 360, to shape the project going forward. The community champions and community participation are integral to making Dragon 360 work where other schemes have failed."

Diane is back at her hotel in central Glasgow. She wants to hold back awhile on the Deep Hole article, and go for a more personal article in the meantime. She reviews the hand written version and proceeds to edit it on her laptop before emailing it to Nick.

Punitive in Action – Precarity in Process

I have lost count of the number of miles I have covered in writing these pieces. What I can say is that it has changed me and my way of thinking and seeing. On a piece of scrubland in Easterhouse in Glasgow I encountered Duncan and his Jack Russell, Minty. This man had worked all his life in one job, on the railways. He had taken pride in his work and he had enjoyed the stability and community it had given him. It gave him a sense of belonging and a connection with the place he lived in. He could see how work had changed, how working class communities have fractured and become disconnected from their surroundings.

Ivan Dunhouse-Jones talked about the need for new jobs when he came to Easterhouse but what people have are zero hours contracts. It's not just a different way of being treated by your employer, but a different way of being, because you are living precariously every day.

Of course we know of cases where bags and pockets are searched on entry to the warehouse, factory or hypermarket, and same on exit. These are no longer people, but human modules who work to the command of the man-machine, packaging things for online shoppers and repackaging them for returns. They are part of an invisible 'non-class' who are only defined by their role in the rise of the "disruptors" – neoliberal business people who know how to rinse the best deal out of a volatile market, where the survival of the fittest is determined by those with the smallest cost base.

The experts have given us new language to describe this – so we have 'The New Precariat' – not a workforce but a commodity of person hours to be costed into a business plan of algorithms. It's a term that dates back to the 1980s in France, defined as a new social class, unprotected by unions and temporary in nature.

While patterns of consumption have changed, our form of government has not. Like an iceberg detaching from the main shelf, the life chances of those entering the workforce now are distinctly different to those of previous generations. But the process of government and policy-making remains isolated from the labour market and social trends, and does not fit where we now are. I say this because – like Ivan Dunhouse-Jones – I have seen it with my own eyes, although I have come to decidedly different conclusions from his. The regulatory systems are now set up to push you into low paid work with zero hours contracts and no security. They are set up to force you to become the human work module, costed into the equation – they are not encouraging you in any way to get a job for life. The job for life does not exist anymore. It is part of a bygone age. But we still live within a culture where, across generations, this is seen as the goal.

So if you get the sense that your life chances are in real trouble, and those of the unborn child even more so, then you are probably right. But what signs are there in Precariat Britain of any fight back?

Perhaps calling it Britain is to imply a unification that is no longer? As our country devolves to Wales, Scotland and the regions, so too do our systems of regulation. We are witnessing a period of great change where more sensitive systems and structures are mandatory. The policy process fails if it ignores those most affected by the policy at hand. Government simply isn't listening to real people and unless this changes, there will be even more disillusionment with politicians and the state. Under politicians like Dunhouse-Jones, government is heading off on a trajectory of selective evidencing from self-appointed campaign groups. In real terms this means that the policy 'wonks' find the data to confirm their 'evidenced' campaigning documents and that becomes post-factual hearsay via the media.

I can see that IDJ must be frustrated that the over-arching effects of globalisation limit the once powerful levers of government in terms of change. Put simply, the 'making work pay' mantra is distant from the heavy loss of blue collar jobs over the last 40 years, as heavy industries have declined. Globalisation has moved economic power away from countries like the UK.

I have however witnessed people who are holding onto the idea of community and the force of local empowerment. They are just no longer relying on the state. I am not naive enough to see this renewed spirit in cooperative working as a cure against the new breed of economic disruptors in online retail connected to zero hours employment contracts.

I have spent several days learning about the Life Chances social enterprise. It is a group of women who are building a business from community values and a shared understanding of what it is like in austerity Britain. They make small runs of jewellery and sell their work online and through other retailers. Many of the members have experienced the brutal intolerance and uncertainty in the way some regulatory systems currently operate. All of the Life Chances members want to work and they also want to put something back in.

I would say that what we need are more flexible resources to encourage this kind of social enterprise. We need more investment and encouragement of people to create businesses that are flexible on their own terms. For example, with childcare and family commitments.

The people of Life Chances in Bristol have demonstrated that work revisited can not only be productive but also restorative. This form of evidence – entrepreneurial activism – draws back power to the collective sensibility and creates a platform for self-determination. The women of Life Chances are not only running their own business, they are reinventing work on their own scale and with dignity.

I keep coming back to the word dignity. It is the state or quality of being worthy of honour or respect. I don't see that in evidence in the regulatory systems or in the wild west of disruptive business, but I do see it at Life Chances in Bristol and when I spoke to Duncan in Easterhouse. Dignity must not only be associated with those who have had the life chances to accrue it, it should be something imbued within our culture. Power to the people!

Chapter 8

September

Nick and Diane sit in *The Image* office discussing the articles that she has produced for the online paper. Nick is very positive about the writing and has some excellent stats to share with her. Nick suggests that they go into a quieter room, as the bustle of people and TV screens are distracting both of them.

"Diane, we really love the work, it's brought in a huge amount of interest from across the board. In August we had a bump on the site which I'm very happy about. We'd like to offer you an extension to take it a bit further, particularly the Wales and Scotland angle. What do you think?" he says.

Diane is delighted it has worked out, but she is all revved up to tell Nick about the call she has received from Toby.

"Nick, I am really up for continuing but there is one thing I need to share with you urgently. I have been in touch again with that guy from G4N, the company that has taken on the Universal Credit roll out. He wants to remain anonymous but I think he has more on what has really been going on. This could be a major scoop for us."

"Ok, what you got?"

Diane reads from her notes. "This is what he said: they brought us in to try and tidy things up but we've found a total mess… manual input of data… lost data… security holes in the software… cost over-runs… invoicing chaos… sign offs for work that appears not to have happened… and people left hanging for weeks on end… it's a complete mess and it's about to be rolled out across the country impacting on millions of people's lives."

"Didn't we run something on this last year? Wasn't Dame Jill Staples on one of the parliamentary committees talking about this? Is it actually a new story, or just a bit more detail on something that's already public knowledge?"

"I checked the records. It did come up in committee, the cost over runs and the IT overspends in particular, but it has not been presented as a joined up story in terms of its impact on the populace at large. This is much bigger than they are saying."

"I am wondering if we are getting off the issue here of devolution and regulatory systems that fit specific communities. For example, the pressure placed on some inner city areas due to immigration. Maybe we need to stay with that?" Nick argues.

"It's all connected, though. If what my source tells me is true, all these communities are about to fall off a bureaucratic cliff. What I've learned from the tour and meeting real people is that many of them don't have a clue about what is going to hit them. The big story is that regulatory systems are designed in isolation from the people who use them. These systems, like Universal Credit, are marshalled through, irrespective of costs, as they serve political ends by communicating and symbolising what this government wants to achieve. The out-sourcing on UC has failed to such an extent that the Department of Work and Pensions were advised to abandon a huge amount of privatised work – millions of pounds. That is the story – the growing disconnect between the working poor and the political establishment..."

Nick is unusually silent and ponders what to do next. "I like the stories of real people in your work, this comes through very strongly. We could take on the government on Universal Credit and run that but ground it in the context of 'real voices'. It is very powerful when you read these compelling stories. Let's leave the specifics of UC alone for a bit and focus in on these. We are now on the run in to the General Election on October 13, so I would like you to bring in some more real voices. I will get you a couple of people to back you up, we have a young woman who is doing some freelance research for us, I'll get her to call you. We can move on Deep Hole after that."

Diane feels deflated. She wants to continue with a wider story and take the readership on a journey through the whole thing. She has to accept that Nick has final say, but that won't stop her from carrying on her own research.

She phones Jonathan and asks him how the Dragon 360 programme is going in Cardiff. She gives him bit of background about her boss's decision to focus in on 'real voices'. She asks him if there are any more people she can interview within the 360 scheme.

"I can't promise anything but I'll see what I can do" says Jonathan.

A day later he texts her and says Amna, whom she met briefly at Northside, is happy to talk to her, but she wants her identity to be hidden. Diane decides to make the journey over to Cardiff again and takes Ellie, the freelance researcher, with her.

At Northside they are greeted by Jonathan who in turns introduces them to Amna and the interpreter Mahnoor. Amna, who looks to be in her early 40s, has a generous smile and a quiet charisma. She wears a pale gold scarf and a long black abaya covering her clothes with black and gold shoes peeking out at the bottom.

“Hello Amna, we’ve met before. Thank you for agreeing to talk to me.” Amna smiles and nods, lightly shaking the hand Diane has proffered. She likes the look of Diane, she seems friendly and she's never met a journalist before.

“Right, let’s go up to the office and talk. It’s private and I can make everyone a cuppa.” Jonathan points the way to the stairs.

Once everyone is settled, tea in hand, Amna begins to tell her story through the interpreter:

“I came to the UK with my husband and our children. We moved from Pakistan to Italy when I was 36 years old. My husband applied for and was granted Italian nationality and I have Italian residency. We spent eight years there before we decided to come to the UK. We have relatives here. When we arrived in Cardiff we first lived with our relatives and my husband got a job working in the Cash and Carry just off Albany Road.”

“What was it like coming to the UK for the first time? How did you become resident here?” Diane asks. Ellie makes notes in the background. Amna is enjoying telling her story.

“I think having Italian nationality helped when we came to the UK, as it was in the European Union. We had to pay a solicitor a lot of money to help us with the application, but now we have five years UK residency and have the right to remain here. We can apply for a UK passport and again we will need to pay a lot of money to a solicitor to make sure we have the right documents and fill in the form correctly. If you get one thing wrong your application is rejected and you have to pay again to re-apply. I am worried now the UK is leaving the EU. I don't know how that will affect my application. My husband works many hours at the Cash and Carry and we don’t see much of him. I don’t work now because we have children but I want to work. I need to improve my English and also I need some training to help me find a job. It was strange coming to Cardiff from Italy, very different. Of course the weather was the first thing we noticed because we arrived here in November.” Amna smiles, remembering how cold she was when she first arrived.

Amna and Mahnoor speak together in Urdu. They have been friends for a while now and she enjoys Mahnoor's company.

"When we first arrived we lived with relatives. There were twelve of us in the house. We had to sleep on the floor and we shared food with my relative. It was very cramped but things got better when my husband got his job. We had some money and we moved out and rented a house. The house is damp and we have to pay £900 per month, which takes up over half of my husband's wage. We send money home to Pakistan whenever we can."

"What kind of problems do you and your family face?" asks Diane.

"We have one son who is disabled and we are trying to get him more help if we can. We need more support to understand the system here, how it works. It keeps changing."

Jonathan talks about the issues that have been raised in the Dragon 360 scheme. He says that the Welsh Government have been very open about how differing immigration status is a part of the overall problem and that many families have complicated immigration backgrounds. Within the pilot programme it had been agreed that a few case studies could be undertaken where non-UK, non-EU participants were accepted, as well as immigrants with EU nationality. Of course this will change, with Brexit, but no-one knows exactly how.

"The issue is that we will never find out how to crack some of these problems, if we don't have these case studies," Jonathan enthuses. "I'm hoping Amna will be able to join the Dragon 360 scheme, but things are totally up in the air with Brexit."

Diane and Ellie leave Northside, thanking Amna, Jonathan and Mahnoor for their time. They take the train from Cardiff Central to Bristol Temple Meads. Across the country political posters appear in front gardens and in fields next to the railway tracks and motorways. Immigration has become the main issue. Ellie spots a Conservative party banner draped across a huge heap of straw bales – 'Families Vote With The Conservatives'.

Desiree, SHE and Shireen have established a steady flow of orders for Life Chances jewellery. Following a two-day session with a consultant they have assessed the supply chain for making the jewellery and how to optimise the process of running an online business. They have reorganised the sessions to allow for discussion with everyone present, then breaking down into small 'production groups'. The result is more jewellery being produced and better quality of the finished items. But they have held on to the communal model and social space, that everyone values.

The final document has been received from EcoEth offering them the £185,000. They have arranged a meeting with all of the Life Chances members to discuss whether to accept it or not. Shireen is strongly in favour but the others are still unsure. She's really frustrated that the others seem to be looking this gift-horse in the mouth. She decides to rewrite the business plan based on accepting the grant but needs help with the figures. At the moment, each member receives an equal division of the profits but it is evident to everyone that some people carry more responsibility than others.

"We need to train up some more people," SHE says.

"And we need to work on the better selling lines," Desiree replies.

"And we need to focus on the campaigning side of Life Chances, we can't forget dat," SHE rejoins.

The group meet at the Life Chances unit. The 'making shifts' are broken down each day to suit the school run, with some people working evening shifts. There are now 24 regular members and they don't have enough chairs for everyone. Surely everyone can see that taking the grant will at the very least give everyone a chair to sit on, thinks Shireen. And better biscuits, she chuckles to herself as she bites into a Rich Tea.

"Thank you everyone for coming, we have lots of important things to discuss tonight," SHE says.

"We have to make some decisions about the social investment offer. We are using model company constitution number two, which means the Directors make the running decisions but the members vote on important things like this. We would all prefer to do this by consensus, that is us all agreeing but that might not happen!" says Shireen.

A long conversation ensues with various differing opinions among the members. Most seem for the grant, no-one has a really strong argument for not taking it. Looks like I was worrying for no reason, thinks Shireen.

"Ok let's have a show of hands," says Desiree, "and then we can see who's for it..."

There is a pause and the majority of members decide to go for the social investment. SHE and Shireen are delighted and Shireen punches the air. Desiree looks vexed and is still uncertain because she doesn't want to expand too fast.

The next item on the agenda is the website. They agree to spend an additional £5,000 on amending the current site, adding in better online purchasing software and inventory control.

Shireen asks everyone if there is any other business. SHE talks about the good press coverage they have been getting. As a result they have been contacted by the Department for Work and Pensions suggesting a visit to Life Chances by Ivan Dunhouse-Jones, no less.

"Basically, I can't stand the man," says Shireen "but it's up to you what we do on this one. I've got my way on the investment money, so I have to be reasonable about this don't I?"

An intense debate takes place and the members are invited to vote. The show of hands is just in favour of IDJ visiting. There is laughter in the room as people begin to wander over to the food table.

"Trust me, I'll be telling him what I think of his policies!" says SHE.

Over at Northside, Phil, from Dragon Welfare, and Jonathan meet up to discuss the Dragon 360 programme. Jonathan is now spending the majority of his time on the programme and asks Phil if he'd like to help out on Dragon 360, with an eye to applying for the paid position on 360 that is coming up in a couple of months. Phil is delighted to be asked, although unsure if he's up to the job. Jonathan persuades him that his skills are just what is needed.

Phil tells Jonathan that he's been trying to get hold of Najma, who had been a regular at Dragon Welfare but he hasn't seen her for a few weeks. Jonathan says that he will ask around the office at Northside.

"We have some very good news too," Jonathan says. "Hadi has been granted leave to stay by the immigration office. She has been told that she will get a national insurance number and she can work. So I'm going to sign her up for 360 too – I reckon she will be able to get work and we can help her with childcare where needed."

Phil is chuffed, he knows how hard it's been for Hadi and her kids. "She'll be made up, that's just the kind of break she needs." Phil takes Jonathan by surprise with a hug, followed by a manly pat on the back. "Champion, Jono. That's just champion."

A week later, Hadi attends her 360 induction interview. There are three people in the room: Jonathan, a senior social worker and an employment advisor on secondment. Jonathan tells Hadi that the interview will take about 30 minutes and then they will agree a 360 plan.

"So, Hadi, can you tell us what you think you need to move things on for you and your family?" Jonathan asks.

"Yes. I want find job that use my skills. I want find house near Ayla's school...because I move now twice and now we have to take two buses to get my daughter to school." Hadi knows that the people in front of her are there to help, but she can't help feeling nervous.

"I understand that you have one good friend here, is that right?" asks the social worker.

"Yes, my Aunt. She has leave to remain. And I have older daughter Ezra. She is at university. She lives in London," Hadi replies.

"How old are your children?" asks the social worker.

"Ezra is eighteen and Ayla is seven."

"Do you have a partner?" asks the employment advisor directly.

"No, no partner," says Hadi, shifting in her seat. She has had so many of these personal questions and wishes she didn't have to keep answering them.

Hadi is grateful when Jonathan picks up on her discomfort and intervenes.

"Hadi, sorry. I know you've probably had it up to here with questions about your personal life. I promise once we've gone through this set of questions, that will be it as far as we're concerned."

Hadi smiles and shrugs. She likes and trusts Jonathan, he has helped her so much already.

"What we need to do is look at the housing situation in the area and continue with the childcare support. We can do a skills audit and look at the training you might need to maximise the chance of finding the right job for you," says Jonathan.

"I would like that," Hadi smiles. She is hugely relieved that she has this support and she can see a window of hope for herself and her family.

Diane meets with Ernst Negri in the British Library on Euston Road in London. It seemed to Diane like a good place to meet an academic, plus they do great coffee in the balcony cafe. And she likes the hushed and studious atmosphere. They sit in a quiet corner and discuss Negri's theories on the future of work.

"My theories are based on an understanding that the workplace and class system have been effectively reordered by the technological age. And this process continues at such a rate that in the near future we will have the equivalent of worklessness, not because of unemployment, but because there is no need for cheap human labour in the way there was in the industrial revolution and post-industrial era. The consequence of artificial intelligence and mechanisation of services will be a new age of paid leisure for what some politicians call the 'working poor'. Perhaps in the middle there will be an economically active professional class and what I am calling an 'operator class'. The professional class will instruct the operator class to control the machines and the artificial intelligences will provide the bulk of the services to the users. We can already see this distinction in businesses in the UK and USA. I have been placed on record as talking about Nile, for example – their factories are devoid of people, they control their inventory through predictive purchasing and automated delivery. They are close to perfecting a non-human supply chain. Even many of the products or so-called 'content' are now created by machines that can analyse huge data sets and provide useful insights to the consumers."

Negri likes to lecture, Diane thinks, even if it's just an audience of one.

"So, what are the humans then – just consumers of products?" she asks.

"This is an interesting existential question that taxes us now, what are humans? Of course we are corporeal, flesh and blood and we have agency that is still in advance of machines. I am often quoted on the process of the task that many people talk about – how does the machine visit the apartment that it has never been to before, find the coffee and then make the coffee with the machine for that? The answer is, such machines need higher sense inputs like that of humans, more complex interleaving of systems and data, to know how to find the coffee in the first place. The machine needs to perhaps sniff the coffee, not just find the bar code in a field of other bar codes," Negri replies.

"And what happens, when the robot can literally smell the coffee?"

"We have these capabilities right now, we have robots that can smell, we are now at the integration point where we are bringing all these things together. It will be possible very soon for artificial intelligences to carry out complex tasks based on real time changes in data."

"I am keen to know what you think of the role of the state and systems of power in this process of artificial intelligence." says Diane.

Negri leans back in his chair, happy to expand on his pet theory.

"The state will adopt more real time systems of gathering data. We have this current obsession with 'the internet of things' but this is just playful productisation of gadgets."

"By internet of things you mean everyday objects like your fridge and your toaster chatting to each other. Sending and receiving data?" Diane interjects.

"Yes, yes." Negri replies with a wave of his hand, slightly annoyed to be stopped in mid-flow.

"The *real* development will be in human-state interfaces which will make our process of governance more fragile or more volatile. The major existential questions lie in this area right now. For example what if the citizen is regulated by sensing devices and tracking equipment? What if voting is conducted from a so called 'smart' watch? We have become accustomed to marginal, interstitial behaviours and spaces. The redundancy of time is an important part of the formative process of life. Children effectively grow from being bored, do they not? It is a short step from 'real time information' gathering for state benefits to full 'real time citizenry', isn't it?" says Negri.

Diane casts her mind back to her trip to Easterhouse. She senses a huge gap emerging between the digital elite and the working poor, struggling against the phenomenal pace of change.

"Professor Negri, my main question is this: will there be poverty in this imagined future you talk about or will basic income guarantee cover the needs of people and their families?"

"This is a very difficult question to answer. We can never place ourselves in a true future, we can only pick up insights from history. I will tell you about a man who was a serial inventor. He went through various ideas and business failures before he came up with something that has changed our world completely. He got into a dispute with one of his backers and then a court case prevailed. He lost the court case and had to abandon the business. This man's name was Johannes Gutenberg and he invented movable type printing in 1440 – that is nearly 600 years ago!" says Negri.

Diane is frustrated. He is more interested in the sound of his own voice than in actually answering her questions.

"But I don't see how this connects to future poverty, Professor Negri?"

"I was coming to that. The arrival of printed type brought about mass communication in Europe and this has now given way to electronic media, which has further increased the speed of communication. The process of literacy was unleashed in the public across Europe because of Gutenberg's invention. Prior to this an elite had power over information and reading. The final stage in this communication revolution will be mass sensing where all things connect. We will see new classes of people emerging around the order and control of data. In sociological terms, uncomfortable problems arise if we have a class of people who do things and make decisions and a class who have things done to them. This is already happening and the people you write about in your work, they are having things done to them through the process of digital state control – that is digital by design for you!" laughs Negri.

Diane checks her phone is still recording. Negri may be slightly pompous and self-aggrandising but he has thought his way into a future that seems highly probable to Diane.

Negri takes a bite of his lemon drizzle cake, wiping his fingers on the paper serviette.

"So will there be poverty in your imagined future?" Diane asks again.

"Basic income guarantee will be a bi-product of mass automation and artificial intelligence. The only counter point to this is mass sterilisation which is unthinkable at this time. There simply will not be enough unskilled jobs to meet the demands of the population, so the economy and lifestyles will need to evolve. Education and skills need to be invested in to create a higher skilled workforce and, if the political masters prefer, there will need to be a form of basic income."

Diane is slightly thrown by his introduction of mass sterilisation into the argument, and that it's unthinkable 'at this time'. When would it ever be 'thinkable' she wonders. And he still hasn't really answered her question about poverty in the future. But he seems certain that basic income guarantee will be imperative rather than optional in his brave new world.

"I am sorry but I must go now. I have a PhD viva to attend this afternoon. I hope you have what you need." Negri gets up and brushes cake crumbs from his trousers, straightens and gives Diane a firm handshake before making his way to the lift.

Diane switches off the recorder on her phone. Her coffee has gone cold. She orders another flat white, retakes her seat and starts writing.

The election campaign gets underway across the country.

The G4N board have called an emergency meeting. Barry knows he's going to face some tough questions from his colleagues. He had toyed with the idea of pulling out, owing to an important 'operational issue', but has decided it is better to face the music.

Craig Tumbleton, the Chairman of G4N, sits at the head of the table and calls the meeting to order.

"Thanks all for coming along today. With the General Election round the corner, I felt it was important to ready ourselves for a range of potential outcomes. Whilst I'm pretty sure the Tories will stay, we need to prepare for the worst case scenario – a change of government. So we need to secure current contracts in readiness."

Heads nod round the table. Even Don Cox looks fairly alert, thinks Barry, not like the previous meeting. But then it is still morning and few hours away from Don's usual liquid lunch at The Savoy Grill.

"We have been looking at the blue skies work of Negri and others in our 'Moon Shot' department and I have invited the department head, Lance Anderson, to brief us on that. Lance, can you give us a quick appraisal on this one, please?"

"Yes, Craig. We are designing a basic income guarantee template for board review in Q1 next year. We have taken on board Negri's work and we are pretty certain that at this stage with the Universal Credit reset we can build in a platform upgrade that would enable this to be rolled out using the same system. We will have something to show you pretty soon. We will, of course, retain the Intellectual Property work on this and work with our excellent team of lobbyists to resell the same system back to government as an upgrade path."

"Excellent, Lance, and well done," says Craig.

"Now, Barry, your item, can you advise us all on Universal Credit and the reset work your team are doing?" Craig's mood has visibly changed. Gone are the smiles and nods he had for good old Lance. A frown passes over his face and he looks into the middle distance as he talks to Barry.

Barry pauses and shuffles through the board papers. It's the moment of truth. He clears his throat, and searching for a friendly face his gaze falls on Baroness Silver.

"The work we are doing has hit a few problems. The ministry have given us two weeks to get the whole package flying. I'll be blunt, Baroness. This can't be done. The audit we carried out shows profound issues across the whole project. Jem has been kind enough to stall things for us at the ministry, but time is now running out. We will need to get them to agree to a staged roll out plan over the next few years. The consequence of going with what we have will be more disaster." Barry sits back in his chair and waits for the proverbial to hit the fan.

"So, we will then incur penalties won't we, Barry, if you fail to meet the milestones?" asks Baroness Sharmi Silver. Not so friendly after all.

"We are, at the moment, looking at a 3 million pound penalty," Barry has decided that it's best to say how it is and face the consequences.

"That is completely unacceptable, Barry. I'm sure I'm not the only one round the table that is having serious doubts about your competency," asks Don Cox.

"I understand your concerns Don. I have our legal department taking the contract to pieces as we speak, and I'm confident that as we inherited a compromised system mangled together by a consortium of IT companies, that we are not liable for any delays in delivery that stem from early system failures. In other words, we adopted a lame donkey and it's not our fault that it limps."

"What about your orange team, why aren't they all over this and sorting it, Barry?" asks Harriet Devonshire-Gables. That's all he needs. A trustafarian with a *friterie* on her shoulder, giving him a hard time.

"My team are all over it, Harriet. They are doing a great job, the deeper they dig, the more they find. So, I've told them to keep digging until they get to the bottom."

"As far as I can see from your recent report Barry, the system is, on the whole, fit for purpose," says Don. "I suggest your team to stop digging and get the damn thing out the door. And I would like to know where the hell that journalist from *The Image* got her information from. And will there be more? Do we have a leak Barry?" He thumps the table for emphasis, spilling his glass of water on Baroness Silver's lap.

Barry takes the handkerchief from his top pocket and hands it over to the Baroness.

"We are looking into that. Some of the information that appeared in her article was known only to a few people in the corporation. I have Human Resources investigating and will have the answer soon."

The articles have unsettled Barry, he has enough on his plate without one of his staff going 'wiki-leaks' on him.

"And Barry, you would be one of the 'few people' which access to that information, am I right?" asks Craig.

"As would you," replies Barry, immediately regretting his words.

Craig is silent for what feels like an eternity.

"Barry, can you leave the room, please?" Craig requests.

Barry senses his days might be numbered. Baroness Silver hands him his now damp handkerchief as he makes his way to the door, shutting it softly behind him.

The board continue the discussion.

"I think we should fire the idiot," says Don Cox.

"I am in favour of pulling his bonus this year and giving him a verbal warning," says Baroness Sharmi Silver.

"Let's take him through to Q4 and then if it all backfires on us with IDJ we can scapegoat him and get rid of him then," says Craig Tumbleton.

The board agree to let Barry continue as a potential sacrificial lamb until the General Election result. They turn to the next item on the agenda, end of year bonuses.

Diane arranges to meet Toby on the South Bank in London. Toby appears in a black hoodie and black jeans, with a black and white bandana wrapped round his face.

Diane can't help but laugh. "Very Anonymous. All you need now is a Guy Fawkes mask and you'll totally fade into the background."

Toby takes off the bandana and shoves it in his pocket.

"Look I came on my BMX, you know what the air pollution is like in London. I'm not trying to look like Anonymous, this is what I normally wear," Toby replies defensively. He had actually come on the tube, bus and by foot (so he wouldn't be followed), and he had started to get into whistleblower chic since he spoke to Diane on the phone, but he wasn't about to tell her that.

"Ok, it is spill time for me,' says Toby, "it's only a matter of time before they rumble me on this."

Diane notes his wording with a smile. Honestly who uses 'spill time' and 'rumble' outside of 1940s film noir? "You mean your employers at G4N?"

"Yeh, big style, well fucked I am. So, questions?" Toby starts fidgeting with his Apple Watch in a way that Diane finds intensely irritating.

Diane decides to take a different slant with her questioning. "What are your life chances comprised of Toby?" she asks.

"Whoa, that's a radical question…let me think…well I played around with gadgets as a kid, spent most of my teenage in my bedroom building a computer from scratch... my old man was in the pharmaceutical industry and he encouraged me to be enquiring…he was a lab technician. I did an MA in Computer Science at Sunderland, where I mainly took drugs and had a laugh…but I came out of it with an excellent understanding of hacking, and shazaam, here I am!" Toby answers glibly.

"My impression of you, Toby, is that you don't have a clue about the lives of people in the real world. Is that the case?" asks Diane.

Toby is unfazed by the question. "What is the real world Diane? I work for a multi-national, they pay me decent wedge and the rest of the time I have fun, that's it – my life chances are all about taking the money and seeing what happens. I can see where you're heading – yes there is a lot of privilege in there but I've earned it."

"So, what do you think about the life chances of the people using the reset version of the Universal Credit system, Toby?" asks Diane.

"Well, to be honest I don't have an opinion on them. I wish them all the best. But, you know, look at the United States – they see our NHS as an evil Orwellian empire – but then people there queue up in a rock stadium for days just to have basic treatment. My point is, your life chances in the UK are probably well better than there, aren't they?"

"So, do you think that people come here because of that?"

"Of course they do, free healthcare, free benefits and free food – what's not to like about that!"

"What benefits do you get currently, Toby?" she asks.

"Nice, got me cornered there. As a Senior VP at G4N I get free private healthcare, eight weeks holiday somewhere hot, access to a private gym and a tasty pension plan. Oh, and continuing work place assessment to help me improve in the job," he replies with a laugh.

"So what happens if you lose this job because of what you tell me?" she asks.

"That is going to happen, I'm sure of that. But with my skills I will walk into another highly paid job even with a bad reference on my CV. People like me are gold dust. May sound arrogant to you, but it's true."

"So, will you go public and on the record about all of this then?" Diane asks.

"Yes, I will," says Toby.

"And why would you do that? Given your admission of total disconnect from the people that will be placed in front of your new system?"

"I am fried, so I may as well go out in a blaze. Like the Sundance Kid. I'll fess up to this because I've been pushed so hard to make it work and I've been up front all the way, but I can see that these drones won't let up. If it becomes public knowledge, I walk away. I can give you a list of geezers who were crocked or fired by this grand scheme and I won't be the last," says Toby.

ASPIRE COURT
£25
N
PEOPL
FIGHTING FO
OUR FUTUR

Chapter 9

October

SHE stands in front of the Life Chances unit with the other women and watches as Ivan Dunhouse-Jones arrives at Aspire Court in his ministerial car. The word must have got out as there is a welcoming party of anti-austerity protestors standing at the gates with placards. Several police officers jostle to hold back the protestors. "They say cut back, we say fight back. They say cut back, we say fight back," the protesters chant.

Someone blows a whistle and a samba band, all dressed in pink, start drumming. IDJ gets out of the car. He is a tall, thin man of around 55 dressed in an expensive suit and with the air of someone used to being in charge. He walks past the protesters, oblivious to their presence, but then stops to listen to the samba band, tapping his foot and smiling. He turns and walks through the gates of Aspire Court, pausing to shake the hand of an attendant policeman. A small coterie of advisors and press people follow in his wake. He is greeted effusively by Roger Moulden, the Chief Executive of Aspire Housing Association. That's the first time I've seen him down here, thinks SHE, as Roger pumps IDJ's hand and starts to guide him over to the live-work units.

After a cursory look at a couple of units, IDJ is ushered over to the women of Life Chances.

"Mr Dunhouse-Jones, this is Life Chances, a social enterprise business making jewellery and set up recently by a group of local women," Roger explains. Someone has done his homework, thinks SHE.

"Excellent, excellent. Pleased to meet you." Dunhouse-Jones holds out his hand to SHE. She looks at his hand and then back at him, not saying a word, and not taking his hand. Dunhouse-Jones, ever the politician, carries on regardless. "And why did you choose this name for your business?" he smiles at SHE.

"I don't need to tell you Minister, where the term Life Chances comes from. Your government takes words out of context and changes them. People in this community are struggling because of your policies, which are limiting their life chances, not expanding them. We called our project Life Chances because we know what life chances people need to thrive – secure jobs with a living wage; good education and healthcare; and the embracing and celebration of cultural diversity. All the things your government are working hard to dismantle."

IDJ's PR people start to look a bit nervous. IDJ just smiles harder. He's been in politics a long time and has the hide of a rhino. He starts to move away from SHE, looking for the next friendly face. He makes a mental note to have a word with the PR company. They really should have vetted the proles he was lined up to meet.

SHE walks alongside him and says, “Five Pathways to Poverty. You make it sound like a lifestyle choice. People are poor because they don’t have any money, not because they are drunk single parents with no GCSEs.”

The PR people and IDJ’s staff quickly step in front of IDJ, blocking SHE from view.

SHE feels pleased she's given the Minister a piece of her mind. She doesn't expect anything to come of it, but she's always going to tell it how it is regardless of who she's talking to.

“How many people work here at the moment?” asks IDJ of the nearest inoffensive looking person.

Desiree, flustered, answers his question on autopilot, not thinking about who she is talking to.

“We have 24 part time people engaged here. It’s not just work they do, it is a community space for people to come together, and talk about how to make change happen,” says Desiree.

“Very impressive, precisely the kind of thing that we want to see more of all over the country. Well done and good luck.”

IDJ turns his back on Desiree and smiles at the camera crew from 'Reflect' who have just arrived. The interviewer asks him the obvious question: who is going to win the election?

“We are feeling confident that the British people will choose success over failure, opportunity over dependency and enterprise over idleness. We know the British people want to get back to work and we want to finish off the important job we’ve started, which is why I am here today.”

IDJ's press people step in and start directing a photo shoot with some of the assembled press photographers. Surrounded by the Aspire management team, Roger, the Aspire CEO, and IDJ do the classic hand shaking pose, turning sideways to smile at the camera.

SHE, unhappy that herself and her colleagues are literally being kept out of the picture, challenges the press photographers. “What about taking a picture of us, the people who work here? We’re the real story, we’re the reason you actually came, remember?”

Another picture is taken, this time including some of the Life Chances workers. This will not be used in any of the media coverage.

Outside, IDJ makes a speech to the gathered press. In the background protestors shout their disapproval. Having quickly recovered from SHE's ambush, he is once again unfazed by the protests and general noise.

“Why did we do this. We’ll look like we agree with the government,” Shireen says pointing at the protestors.

“It is small businesses like this one that represent hope in our communities. Everyday people, going about their business, transforming lives and tackling worklessness. Part of the story of our great country is enterprise and willingness to take risks. What I’ve seen today at Aspire Court gives me great hope for the future. The ladies of Life Chances, whom I met today, are taking up the challenge of moving from state dependancy to entrepreneurial gain. To quote the great philosopher of the free market economy, Adam Smith, 'The real tragedy of the poor is the poverty of their aspirations.' But here today I have met a very aspirational group of ladies proving that wrong. Thank you ladies, and well done.” IDJ smiles in Desiree's general direction before moving swiftly to his waiting Jaguar XJF.

The media circus packs up rapidly and heads off towards IDJ’s next appointment at Vapid Aeronautics, a company supplying laser systems to the military. The Life Chances workers watch as everyone peels away, including the protestors.

“I can't believe what that man just said!” SHE spits, fuming at IDJ's patronising comments.

Desiree and Shireen just look at her, lost for words.

Najma is at home in Cardiff, having returned from dropping off her daughter at school. The morning post arrives and she receives a letter from the General Medical Council confirming that she can practice as a doctor in the UK. She is delighted and tearful at the same time.

She has gone through a lot to get to this point and could not have achieved it without the help of Dragon 360.

She examines the certificate and it feels like control of her life chances is now within her own hands: "United Kingdom, Certificate of Completion of Training, Dr Najma Jibril, Speciality General Practice."

The following day she meets up with Jonathan at Northside for a review of her progress. She shows him the certificate and they both become emotional.

"I am delighted, Najma, this means so much – it is an example of what can be done if we work together," Jonathan says.

"I want to thank you and your colleagues for your help. I will be able to get some locum work in the next few weeks and that is all because you connected me to the right people," says Najma.

Jonathan puts in his monthly report to Dragon 360. He highlights Najma's breakthrough as an achievement for the scheme. He emphasises the importance of joined up working and how face-to-face work has enabled her to build her confidence and feel as if she is supported.

Najma begins work in a small surgery in Cardiff and talks to Jonathan about setting up a clinic and counselling service aimed at asylum seekers and new migrants.

Diane is working at home on the next article in her Life Chances series. She is thinking about Nick's comments, on leaving Universal Credit alone and concentrating on different circumstances for people living in the UK. With the general election only a week away, she needs to get a piece out that connects life chances with the electoral manifestoes. She decides to call IDJ's office at the ministry for a quote, knowing that she will receive standard election patter from the press department. To her surprise the ministry press office redirects her to one of IDJ's advisors, who agrees to a phone interview on the basis of being quoted only as a spokesperson.

"Well, I am surprised to get through to someone," says Diane. Jem has heard whisperings that *The Image* is working on a big Universal Credit story, and whilst he didn't usually take calls from freelance journalists, he wants to get a feel for who he is dealing with.

"This is Jem Devine, I am one of Ivan Dunhouse-Jones's advisors," Jem replies.

"Can I ask you some questions about current policy?" asks Diane.

"Sure, fire away," says Jem, looking at a photo of Diane he's pulled up on his computer. Not exactly his type, he thinks, but not bad. Kind of feisty looking.

"Can you tell me why you've taken this call? It's not normally the case that we can get hold of anyone in your department so quickly."

"We are big fans of open government here and we have nothing to hide," Jem replies breezily, scrolling through Diane's online CV.

"Ok. Can you tell me about the planned roll out of Universal Credit. How long is it going to take?" Diane queries.

"Diane. It is Diane, isn't it?" Jem smooches down the phone.

"Yes that's right." There is something about Jem's voice that sets Diane's teeth on edge.

"Diane, we have held many press conferences on that topic. I would have thought your editor would have told you that's old news now. UC is being rolled out around the country as we speak. That really is all there is to it."

Jem's voice is hyper friendly, Diane can almost hear him grinning down the phone. She pushes again. "Why won't you talk about UC?"

"I am extremely happy to talk about Universal Credit, Diane. It is the flagship project for IDJ and our department. But there really isn't anything new to say at the moment," says Jem.

Diane can't get past his stonewalling, so, adopting Jem's pseudo-friendly tone, she tries a different tack.

"Jem, you obviously have your ear to the ground. Could I ask what things you think affect people's life chances right now in the UK?" smiles Diane.

"Great question, now we're getting somewhere, I would say that jobs, education and the family are all foundation points of someone's life chances."

"And what if they don't have any of those?"

"Well, it's our role in government to help them find a job, help them educate themselves and make a good strong family unit."

"I have met a considerable number of people over the last six months, Mr Devine, and what I've seen is a new form of precariousness. For example in Easterhouse, where there has been some regeneration but people still have no job security. What is your view on this?"

"IDJ has a lot of affection for the people of Easterhouse since his visit in 2009. We believe that by providing support for people in work we can change their lives which of course means their life chances."

"So, what about work? What kind of jobs are there for people without skills?" asks Diane.

"Diane, you know we want it to pay to be in work and we are doing all we can to create jobs in places like Easterhouse. But there is a gap in terms of skills. We quite simply have got to get more skilled people into the economy and workforce."

"What do you think when you see people from other countries filling the skilled jobs and local people not able to get into the skilled workforce, Mr Devine?"

"IDJ's opinion is that we need skilled jobs for British people and where necessary we in-fill with non-UK nationals."

"Do you think you're going to win the election, Mr Devine?" asks Diane.

"Yes, we are confident we will win, there isn't really anybody substantial up against us is there, Diane?"

This guy is a total jerk, thinks Diane. She thanks him for his time, not quite able to keep the insincerity out of her voice. She returns to her computer and starts writing her next article, Jem's slimy patter spurring her on.

Jem sits for awhile at his desk. He drops an internet scavenged photo of Diane into the Nudifier app on his iPhone and starts painting off her clothes.

Smoke and Mirrors

I once more return to the words of life chances. What I mean is commonly now being termed in the media as post-factual analysis. Or, do we mean making it up as you go along to suit yourself? This is deeply troubling, the construction of a new truth - yes, Orwellian in every way.

As you know, I have been following IDJ's footsteps across the country, meeting real people and gaining an insight into their worlds – insights that IDJ must have had too. I found myself wondering if this was some pre-planned ideological tactic to confirm judgement on these people. But I don't think IDJ is that cynical, I think he was disturbed by what he saw – but then transported back to the pressure tank of Westminster and its privilege of thought. Why did IDJ seize upon life chances as a mantra? Of course he knew that to change the system, you have to change the language and this he has done.

Most sane commentators I've spoken to agree that there is a huge gap between government espousals of new life chances indicators and the reality of increased poverty. Put plainly, a forward party of government agents are not going to improve the day to day life of an adult or child in Glasgow, Cardiff or Bristol based on these words alone. They will need proper resources – time, money and scale.

The mist of weasel words cannot hide the gradual impact of austerity in its physical form – the closure of children's centres, freezing child benefit and changes in how child poverty is defined. We are days away from the next General Election when the electorate will have the choice to adopt the language of smoke and mirrors or vote for something else – perhaps another kind of smoke and mirrors!

The objective on my journey has always been to unpack the language of IDJ's crusade and reconnect it with real situations, literally test it against real life chances. It is not uncommon now for terms like 'life chances' to be used as a particular political medium, a sleight of hand. After all, despite the origins of life chances in Marx, we now have centre-right politicians adopting those concepts and fluidly developing them in questionable form. They twist the language and that is cruel and disrespectful to the genuine people that I met.

The eminent sociologist, Peter Townsend effectively argued that poverty denies people the opportunity to participate fully in society. If we want people to take back control over their lives then we still have to recognise the role of the state in shaping the places we live.

You need access to money and resources to acquire agency in the economy in the first place. If you don't have it you are at the state's mercy. All of my experience following in IDJ's footsteps suggests that there is a clear contradiction in withdrawing key services that enhance interaction and agency while proclaiming the enhancement of life chances as a working political mantra. So, participation and agency then link back to community and cohesion because citizens make a positive investment in their place. Participation then leads to social status, social capital, well-being and respectful interaction.

If IDJ was to return to Easterhouse, he would find the people embittered and worn down by austerity - not yet broken - but inevitably feeling the disconnect between the actuality of the place that they are in and the empty rhetoric of narrow gauge conservatism.

The key dividing factor in these centre-right ideologies is one of choice as the Joseph Rowntree Foundation pointed out in their excellent 'Poverty, Participation and Choice' report (2013). In this instance a key indicator of social status and value in terms of life chances is in the form of participation in social and cultural activities that an individual or peer group undertakes. Greater income and security raise levels of choice, from those connected to essential goods, such as food, to more consumable items associated with 'status'.

It follows that as income falls, so does choice and participation. In the Tory version of life chances, our notional individual – let's call him Stephen – will not choose to go down the Pathway to Poverty, but will walk on by and take the 'right' path to economic prosperity. He will see the benefit of work, rise up the earning scale and feel the gradual cushion (or taper) peel away as he stands on his own two feet. The taper is another term to describe effective withdrawal of benefits as income increases.

Does Stephen wish for a new iPhone or does he want to develop social cohesion in his community? Or does he want both? On his journey he might be faced with conflicts of agency as an 'actor in the field' – does he campaign to save the local library or do extra shifts at the sports packaging factory for more money?

The Rowntree report homes in on Townsend's use of the word

'breakpoint' to describe the disproportionate drop away in participation that occurs in poverty. So, to utilise a common term in ready use – there is no 'taper' in participation there is a complete drop. People are in poverty so they do not participate in the social and cultural fabric of the places they live. They are economically shut out.

Pushing the same terminology into matters of the state, we can now argue that there is a steeper 'taper' in terms of what it provides and does not. That is poverty, like it or not, when things drop away from you, or are out of your reach.

Down the long corridor of lonely life chances, we hear the echo of the patriarchal voice murmuring "but we have to live within our means". One thing however that we can thank IDJ for is opening up a plural debate – even if I don't agree with him, I now have a renewed sense of urgency in contesting these weasel words and spirals of language.

The penny has truly dropped in writing this today. The taper idea in life chances, and its connected schemes, is built on an idea of the individual as an economic unit, while the theories of people like Latour and Bourdieu chart the wider array of social capital and social space, fundamental in co-existence within a community. So, hidden within the words of life chances is a neo-conservative rehash of Thatcherite ideas.

In Glasgow, Easterhouse, I found this strongly expressed in interviews with local people. There are barriers to participation and misunderstandings of what the state intends because the likelihood is that Scotland will go its own separate way.

In Townsend's research, poverty and deprivation are measured by financial concerns, housing, health and living conditions. In the new incarnation of life chances, poverty is remade as we have said around the causality of the Pathways to Poverty – family breakdown, educational failure, worklessness, benefit dependency, addiction and debt.

I found a circle of solidarity in the women of Life Chances, the social enterprise making jewellery and creating hope in Bristol. This socially minded business displays an emerging agency and collectivisation of people towards multiple goals. This agency is leading to connections, personal development and increased confidence. The investment required to do something like this is small when compared to other government schemes.

One thing that has stuck with me is the plight of the Somali asylum seekers I met in Bristol. I tried to contact the mother and her five year old daughter, but they disappeared. Things like this leave you wondering exactly what happened.

If you have a chance, go and see Life Chances jewellery for yourself. *https://www.etsy.com/uk/shop/LifeChances*

Mona and Samira are informed by immigration services that they are to be rehoused, not in Bristol but in Cardiff. At short notice they gather their belongings and go to the bus station. Mona knew they wouldn't be able to stay with Asha for long, not with all the trouble her and Abdi have been going through, but she didn't expect to have to move cities. Once in Cardiff they have been told to go to the Somali Advice Centre in the west of the city.

Samira sits on the wheely suitcase Mona has borrowed from Asha, and Mona pulls her the final mile from the bus stop to the centre. The going is slow, the October wind cutting through their thin clothing. Neither of them has a decent winter coat. Mona just wants to stop moving. She thought they would make a home in Bristol, where she has family. She never imagined she'd have to move to a different country where she knows no one. At the centre they sit waiting for someone to see them. A man appears and they begin to talk in Somali. He calls a taxi and instructs the driver in Somali to take them to their new home. The taxi driver does this for free and helps them unload the luggage at the new address. They are met by a man who passes the keys to Mona. The keys are stiff in the lock and he helps them in getting in. The hallway is dark and there are children's toys and black bin bags spread across it. There is a strong smell of damp and wood chip wall paper peeling off the walls.

They enter the small front room and there is more detritus from the previous tenants. A settee is overturned and an armchair is covered in a colourful throw. In the kitchen, the fridge door is ajar and a small stove is caked in burnt food. An aluminium pan contains the remains of the last meal cooked.

Mona's eyes well up and Samira hugs her tightly. They stand like that for a while, the daughter comforting the mother, until Samira starts wheezing. The little girl's asthma is triggered by the damp conditions. Mona finds Samira's inhaler in her handbag and watches as she breathes in the medicine and the wheezing subsides.

They bed down for the night in the cold room upstairs. The house feels dark and unwelcoming.

The system is full of similar people and it has no human face. Mona knows they are lucky to be offered this place, even though they have no idea where they are. Just as she thought their journey was over, they have been moved on again.

In the morning they go out with the small amount of money they have and buy breakfast. They return to the Somali Advice Centre and speak to one of the workers about Samira's asthma. The woman is kind, bringing hot food to the mother and child. She tells them about a doctor Samira can see for her asthma. She gives her the details of the refugee clinic that is being set up by Dr Najma Jibril.

Mona and Samira return to their small house and begin to make it feel like home. The little girl helps her mother clean the kitchen and in the late afternoon the gas is switched on so that they can cook. A volunteer knocks on the door from the Somali association and delivers a food box. He gives her the name of a man called 'Phil' who runs a food bank and draws her a map on how to get there. Mona feels more positive. There are people who care, even if the system fights against them.

Desiree finishes mopping the floors in the lower deck area of the G4N Bristol building. It's her final day and as she puts the equipment away for the last time and makes sure everything is clearly labelled for the new cleaner. She takes a look at the Deep Hole servers whirring away in their racks. Though they treated me like a dog, she thinks, I'm going to miss this place and de sound of the machine.

She turns round to be presented with a cake by Derek, the sysops guy.

"That's very kind of you Derek, I didn't expect anything like this!"

"I asked up in HR and they said you've been here for five years. I think you deserve some acknowledgment of that, don't you?" says Derek.

"Well, thank you," she says. Desiree is touched by the fact that Derek has remembered that chocolate fudge cake is her favourite.

"I did a bit of a whip round in the office and there's a card here for you," Derek says.

She opens the card and inside is a Debenhams voucher for £50.

"I really can't believe it, some of de staff would just walk past mi, and nuh say hello let alone give mi money. So I'm surprised. But I've been praying you know, and I'm starting mi new business, and look now, God bless me with money."

"The top brass have signed it too, look there's Eddie's signature at the bottom."

Desiree reads the names on the card, mostly people she's never met. But it is the thought that counts she thinks. Helen from HR appears and thanks Desiree for all of her work.

"You've been our best cleaner by far, Desiree, we've never had anyone so thorough as you and you're a hard act to follow. I'm sure you're going on to greater things with your new business venture, I didn't realise we had a budding entrepreneur in our midst! I do need that pass off of you though, we don't want an AAA pass getting into the wrong hands do we?" Helen laughs.

Desiree hands the AAA pass to Helen. Wha she know about mi? thinks Desiree, de woman never met mi before. Desiree lets it pass. She's out of here now and onto something that actually uses her skills.

Derek gives Desiree an awkward hug. "Stay in touch won't you?" he says, blushing slightly.

"I will. You always nice to me and respected me Derek, I love that. So look after yourself, don't make the brutes work you too hard," Desiree replies.

Derek excuses himself and enters the Deep Hole server room. He has been told that there is another big upgrade coming down the line and to prepare for a lot of extra work.

He hasn't told anyone, but Deep Hole has started making the groaning noises again. Sometimes, when Derek stays late, it sounds like Deep Hole actually forming words amidst the groaning. Derek tries to reassure himself that it's just his imagination. Too many late night horror movies.

Diane defies Nick's advice and arranges to meet Toby again. This time they meet at a Turkish restaurant around the corner from The Globe Theatre on the South Bank. The stone paving is slippery underfoot and Diane shifts over to the paved area. A group of Japanese tourists pose for selfies with The Globe behind them.

Toby arrives late and dramatically passes a dossier of documents across the table to Diane. She opens it up and finds copies of invoices, print outs of emails and headed official documents from the Department of Work and Pensions.

"It's all there, enjoy!" Toby says, obviously pleased with himself, "it's a bit like a scene from a scandi-thriller, isn't it?"

Diane scans through the file. She picks out several emails from Jeremy Devine, the creepy guy who stonewalled her on the phone, all to G4N Orange Team personnel. She reads them and smiles. There is enough information to develop a full scoop and she hopes she can persuade Nick to go for it. If he doesn't, she'll go to *The Telegraph*, as they seem to have people over everything connected to government impropriety. She had been hoping this scoop would lever her into Nick's job, or at least one at a similar level and with the same security. But working for *The Telegraph* would be ok too, even if it didn't quite reflect her politics. In either case, her life was going to change for the better, she was sure of that.

"This is the guy I spoke to yesterday, Jeremy Devine, he's right in the middle of this story isn't he?"

"Oh yes, he is the bag man, not to be crossed at all – Jem to his mates. This guy gives hairdryer treatment that would make Sir Alex Ferguson wince."

Diane reads an email from Jem to Barry Hamilton, marked high importance. It is full of strong words urging G4N to sort out Universal Credit.

"So, is there anything else I need to know?" asks Diane.

"You need to know that at one point the system was running on spreadsheets, like Excel. It still cracks me up, thinking about poor old people in the DWP having to keep their mouths shut and use Excel, while the biggest amount of money ever spent on IT was passing them by. What a fucking disaster!" says Toby with mirth and obvious release written all over his face.

"Why did that happen?" asks Diane.

"Because the whole thing was being pushed too fast and the preparation was inadequate. Some guy was emailing around and putting up a campaign saying that face-to-face would have been cheaper and more humane. Well he was right, it would have been a lot easier – when you look at the invoices and money, you'll see it's off the scale. You could have interviewed everyone for Universal Credit in Ibiza and still come in with some spare."

"Thank you, Toby, I really appreciate what you've done."

They finish their lunch and chat about what Toby will do next, once he's fired.

"Don't worry, I'm going to leave before I'm pushed." Toby zips up his hoody and says his goodbyes. He refrains from putting on the bandana he has in his pocket – at least until he is outside.

Debra drives Secnach to the bus terminal. After six months they have become good friends and agree to keep in touch.

"We're a bit early, d'you want to get a coffee or something to eat?" Debra asks.

They drive round the Bear Pit roundabout and Debra parks up her car.

"I've bought you a little gift to take home with you, Secnach," Debra says, as they sit in the coffee shop looking out at the early autumn rain.

Secnach opens the small box and pulls out a mug inscribed with the legend 'We Make Our Own Futures', made by the People's Popular Republic of Shapeshifters.

"When you're back on your island, you'll be able to have a lovely cup of tea and think of us here in Bristol," Debra says. Secnach looks at the mug and smiles. She doesn't drink tea but is too polite to mention it.

"I haven't forgotten what you said, Secnach, about cultural differences. I've learnt so much from you in this short time. I wish you could do some more work with our newer staff members. Some of them still need more equality and diversity training," Debra gushes.

"I too have learnt much from you Debra. Thank you for helping me with my research. I have lots to write about."

Debra sheds a tear as she hugs Secnach before she gets on the bus. The bleep of the reversing bus bounces off the neighbouring wall and they wave at each other.

Secnach falls asleep on the bus from Bristol to Heathrow. In 48 hours she will be back in the paradise of Zantonica, with a new job awaiting her.

The election results start to come in at 22:48pm on the 13th of October. The sitting Labour candidate wins Houghton and Sunderland South.

Jem and Barry sit together watching the television in Barry's office at G4N. Barry didn't actually want to be socialising with Jem. The more they worked together, the more Barry disliked him. There was something perverse about Jem that Barry couldn't quite put his finger on. Jem had been a bit of a slimy toad when they were at Dragon School. Barry hadn't bothered to keep in touch with him after they'd gone up to Oxbridge. Now he remembered why.

There had been a bomb threat on the Jubilee Line and the underground was at a standstill. The streets were still packed with disgruntled commuters and anti-terrorist police. There was no way either of them were getting out of there any time soon.

"If we win then I am hoping to get a new government position," says Jem. "Maybe Director of Communications at Culture or Trade. Hopefully not Communities and Local Government. Now there's a thankless task if ever there was."

"If you win, I'm hoping we'll get a further extension on four of our major contracts," says Barry, refilling Jem's wine glass. He walks over to his desk and tops up his own glass. He looks out of the window at the maze of emergency vehicles below, their flashing lights adding a festive feel to their terror activities. He wishes they would hurry up so he could get away from Jem and back home to his wife.

"We've put you forward for a gong, Barry. Don't mention it to anyone but you should be at least OBE, maybe a bit higher."

"But what about the Universal Credit issue, surely that will affect things?" asks Barry, unnerved by the gift Jem has laid before him.

"Oh no, Barry, you've done your time old chap, I wouldn't worry about that."

Barry is relieved that Jem has cooled on the roll-out plan. Maybe Jem has some knowledge that he doesn't? Or could it be that they have persuaded the ministry to take a longer run at the pilot stage?

Barry pours himself some more wine "Cheers, here's to old...erm... friends," Barry says as they clink glasses.

They watch as more results come in. Barry is surprised that so many of the Labour candidates are going down in Northern marginals – but then the figures suggests a swing over to UKIP.

Barry falls asleep on the sofa in the office, as Jem watches the latest result from Thurrock. Another one for UKIP: that's 20 now. So, the swing finally happened.

Jem wakes Barry up at 3am in the morning.

"Who won?" asks Barry.

"It looks like it will be us, Barry, but there's been a huge swing over to UKIP and Scotland is going off on one."

They order a taxi and head home. In the morning pundits agree that it is going to be a Conservative government, by a margin.

Chapter 10

November

Diane arranges a meeting with Nick and Dan Boothroyd-Wright, the Editor of *The Image*. She is nervous about how they will respond to the information and dossier she is going to present them. Working with Ellie, the researcher, she has tried to cross check all of the insider documents against known public statements on Universal Credit. They now have a full picture of how the public statements differ from the internal communications. Dan strolls into Nick's office with a mug of coffee and reading glasses dangling around his neck. He is in his mid-fifties and well respected among colleagues for his open style of management.

Diane gives them copies of the dossier and watches as they leaf through.

"Diane, what do you think we should do with this? Front page paper, with inside commentary, or online tarted up photo story with breakout points – or maybe Saturday magazine 4-pager?" says Dan, magnanimously.

"Definitely front page, Dan. With a double page spread inside. I really like the block yellow you've been using on the masthead recently, to signal a big story. I think we can play around with it graphically to really grab people's attention," says Diane.

"Nick, what do you think?" says Dan.

"Yeah, sure, front page definitely. It's dynamite." Nick replies, winking at Diane.

Diane can now see that what felt like Nicks endless prevaricating was just him pushing her. Still, he could have been a bit more upfront, she thinks, she's not some rooky reporter from the sticks.

"Ellie, what's your opinion?" asks Dan, sitting on the desk next to Ellie and smiling intensely. He is such an old school flirt, thinks Diane.

Ellie is taken aback by his obvious flirting. It's not the kind of workplace behaviour she is used to. She stands up and looks down at Dan.

"I think Diane's done a great job of getting this and she's been amazing in travelling in the footsteps of IDJ. I would go for front page and copy what *The Telegraph* do, you know drip feed it out over a period of weeks to cause the maximum amount of damage and gain the maximum amount of readers…" says Ellie.

"Ellie I think you may have come up with the approach, well done. Have we got you on the firm yet? Or still freelancing?" says Dan.

"I'm freelancing here two days a week and one day a week on HoneyHaunches," replies Ellie.

"HoneyHaunches, what a fascinating name. What is HoneyHaunches may I ask?" Dan queries, trying another ham-fisted attempt at flirting.

"It's a feminist online zine dedicated to the eradication of cis-centred postlapsarian factriarchy," Ellie says, straight faced.

Diane can see Dan is slightly bewildered by Ellie's reply.

"Right, ok. Thanks Ellie. Erm...Nick, what's your view on drip feed?" says Dan.

Nick is not pleased with the idea, he has a firm conviction in critical journalism and despises *The Telegraph*'s approach. He doesn't want to copy them.

"Whilst it's an excellent scoop, I would still like to run it within the wider story around life chances," he says bluntly.

"I know, let's do a comparator of ten people from Diane's research and do one of those wonderful infographics that that American woman does…you know Wendy Rogers…pricey I know, but we could run that in the paper and online. I love Wendy Rogers's work. And we can drip feed the Universal Credit story over four weeks. It will give the returning government something to play with. Do we know who else is on this, Diane?"

"Nobody else has it, just us," replies Diane.

"Great stuff. Ok, so all agreed then. Wendy Rogers infographic and drip feed exposé over four weeks. Maybe we can pull at least one resignation from this, eh?"

Dan wanders out of the office, casting a wistful glance at Ellie as he leaves. Nick gets back to his computer, looking through his contacts for Wendy Roger's email address. Diane wonders if he knows she's gunning for his job. He looks up from his screen and smiles at her. She feels guilty, but only for a moment.

At Aspire Court, Shireen and SHE have been locked in the small office for the day with Shelia and Tamsin from *Play Fair*, a business consultancy specialising in social enterprises. They have been developing a revised business plan and financial projections. Both SHE and Shireen know that they need help in managing the expansion but are mindful of keeping a balance between profitability and staying true to the spirit of their enterprise.

"The management accounts need to reflect the picture over the next six months and give you guidance on where the business is going," says Sheila, a softly spoken woman in her mid-forties with a fashionably asymmetrical haircut.

"The problem you have is that you've got a lot of asset locked up in inventory and you need to look harder at the market," says Tamsin, who enjoys playing bad cop to Sheila's good cop. She clasps her hands in front of her, the chunky silver rings lined up along her fingers look like knuckle dusters. She nods towards the jewellery laid out on the desk.

"You see these, circular cut acrylic ones, they are making you more money than the fancy ones that people spent more time on, that's because you're able to turn them out quicker and there are less parts," says Tamsin pointedly.

"Wait a minute – we are running something here to develop people's talent, confidence and self value, it's not just a factory approach you know?" says Shireen, narrowing her eyes. Tamsin knows that if they're not successful business-wise, the socially minded aspect of what they are doing will fall apart.

"How about talking with the members about the balance of time spent on pieces versus what is actually selling?" asks Sheila.

"Or we could change the pricing structure for the more fancy pieces?" says SHE. Tamsin can see that SHE is unfazed by her bad cop routine and is a natural business woman. She smiles and nods.

The current procedure on pricing is that the maker sets the price of the item. They then bring this to the pricing group and everyone agrees the final price. Most items are selling for £10, competing with High Street fashion prices, but they have sold a complicated necklace for as much as £80.

They decide to call it a day and Sheila and Tamsin head off to another meeting across town. SHE and Shireen discuss with Desiree what they can do about pricing. Desiree agrees that they should stick to what they know and price things to match the High Street, plus a bit added on because it's handmade. SHE doesn't think they've heard anything from Shelia and Tamsin they didn't already know, but sometimes it is useful to have what you are thinking said out loud, by someone else.

Life Chances recently appeared in the *New Statesman* in an article on community run businesses. There were pictures showing the various jewellery lines and a link to the Life Chances website and Etsy selling page. The business received a surge in orders from all over the world and some items are out of stock.

"I think we should take on the other unit, Shireen, what you saying?" asks SHE.

"Yes, we need more space just to store all of the packaging, don't we?" says Shireen.

"Mi feel nice bout dis, I never expect it to move so fas. We can't forget why we set this up, to challenge the government policies that are limiting the life chances of our community," says SHE.

Barry is sitting in his office when Jane brings in the letter he has been waiting for. Jane of course usually deals with all his mail, but people talk, and the parliamentary seal and heavy embossed envelope acts as a pretty good indicator of its contents.

He takes his silver letter opener off the desk and slices the envelope cleanly. He reads:

Cabinet Office, Ceremonial Officer IN CONFIDENCE
Dear Mr Hamilton,

The Prime Minister has asked me to inform you, in strict confidence, that having accepted the advice of the Head of the Civil Service and Main Honours Committee, he proposes to submit your name to the Queen. He is recommending that Her Majesty maybe graciously pleased to approve you being awarded an Order of the British Empire (OBE).

Barry places the letter on the table, slightly dejected. He had hoped it might be a CBE.

News spreads around the office of Barry's award. His staff congratulate him effusively. Word on the office grapevine was he was heading towards a golden kiss-off, but with an OBE coming his way, they reckon he'll be around for a while longer.

Barry phones Jem to tell him the news.

"It's an OBE, Jem, like you said."

"Well done, very well deserved. I was pushing for a CBE but the PM has decided to go popular and doled them out to ageing actors and pop stars."

"I suppose the Universal Credit debacle hasn't helped things either, has it?"

"Oh, we're generally not bothered about that kind of thing," says Jem "a bit of failure doesn't affect the gong department at all. I do need you to sort that matter out though – we are literally out of time Barry, aren't we? Or should I say, aren't you?"

Barry reaches into his top desk and gets out the Gaviscon. He is well on his way to an ulcer.

"The big news is that IDJ has retained the DWP job and I'm moving onwards and upwards."

"Yes I heard you've been moved to Communities and Local Government. Bit of a sideways move, eh?" Barry is unable to keep the smile out of his voice. At least Jem has got what was coming to him. Not without passing the buck onto Barry on his way out, though.

The call is interrupted by Barry's PA, Jane, entering the room.

"It is urgent, Barry, really urgent!" Barry sees a look of panic on her face. What now?

He reluctantly ends the call before he can really rub Jem's nose in it.

"Barry, Barry, Toby has resigned and disbanded the Orange Team en masse – they have all just walked out…" says Jane.

"What, they can't do that, why didn't I hear about this sooner?"

"Because Toby has just fired off an email to everyone, saying we are, please excuse my language, 'fucked' and he's off."

"Get him on the phone NOW," Barry commands. The phone rings and goes through to voicemail: "You've reached Toby Thomas. I don't listen to voicemails but I do respond to emails..."

"I'll give him something to respond to." Barry leaps up out of his chair and strides towards the lift, his blood boiling. He pushes through the security doors on Orange floor and enters the reception. Dom the receptionist is sitting forlornly at his desk.

"Where is Toby?" shouts Barry.

"They've left, all of them. All I know is that they have had an offer to work for KZM Closters. Toby told me to stay here and manage the backload but obviously I can't do that, can I?"

"But they are under contract. They can't leave, we'll bloody sue them..."

"Toby told me that they've exercised the release clause in their contracts. He said you would understand, it's to do with impropriety..." Dom is sheepish.

"Impropriety!" shouts Barry. "I'll have his fucking head on a stick by the end of the day."

Barry is hyper-ventilating. He sits down on one of the pink sofas. Holding his head in his hands, he tries to compose himself.

He rises from the sofa and heads back to his office. Frantic phone calls ensue but no-one can track down Toby.

Jane enters the room, her anxiety growing by the minute. "Sorry, Barry, I've got some even worse news. You know that young lady from *The Image*, she's on the phone. I think you'd better take it."

"I can't talk to the fucking press now, Jane, tell her to call back later!"

"She says they are about to run an exposé on Universal Credit, would we like to comment?"

Barry can't believe that this is all happening on the same day.

"Yes!" he shouts down the phone at Diane.

"We are going to run a piece on the Deep Hole contract and G4N's involvement in it. Do you remember I interviewed you earlier in the year?" says Diane, infuriatingly calm.

"Yes, I do remember you, of course I do, and I am warning you that you will be looking at one bill and a half of legal damages if you do this," shouts Barry, as he starts working his way through the packet of Gaviscon.

"We have some internal documents, passed on to us by a whistle blower that show exactly what has been going on. Cost over-runs, Excel spreadsheets and huge sums signed off on work for Deep Hole. But G4N actually comes out ok, you look like you're trying to clean up on a bad job, which is why I wondered if you have anything to add Mr Hamilton?"

"Do not run this, leave it alone," says Barry.

"No comments?" says Diane.

"No comment," says Barry and slams down the phone.

He spends the rest of the day in his office with G4N lawyers pouring over the Orange Team contracts. It appears that there is a clause around malpractice. The lawyers advise that there is nothing that Barry can do, apart from reminding the Orange Team of the intellectual property clauses in each of their contracts.

The following day, Jane receives a bombardment of calls from newspapers and suppliers responding to the tip-off that something is not right at G4N. Employees are reminded of their duty of silence and Friends PR arrive to discuss a defensive strategy for the company.

"It is tricky, isn't it?" says Julia from Friends PR, picking off some invisible lint from her Chanel suit.

Barry wonders if the retainer they pay Friends PR is actually doing anything more than just keeping Julia in designer clothes. He has instructed Jane to bring in Michelle Wolff Associates, who have a reputation for defensive PR work.

"We recommend you put out a release, emphasising G4N's role in organising the 'reset' and the solid progress that you have achieved working under difficult circumstances."

"And what do we say about the mass resignation and defection of the Orange Team to KZM Closters?" asks Barry, his voice heavy with sarcasm.

"Well, that is tricky too. But we generally recommend that you point out that they've been offered more money and more perks, so then it looks like they are being greedy."

Barry nods in exasperation and Julia is dismissed to get on with it. He pops another Gaviscon.

Amna and Najma are waiting at the school gates. They greet each other as a way of showing respect and acknowledging the connection they have.

"Asalamu Alaikum," says Amna.

"Walalhu Salaam," replies Najma.

Amna knows Najma through her children, and she has seen Najma in meetings with Jonathan at Northside. They talk slowly as Amna's English is not as good as Najma's yet. Najma tells Amna about her qualifying as a doctor and setting up a clinic for asylum seekers and refugees. Amna is impressed by this achievement. She wishes she knew what work she would like to do. She has spent most of her life looking after her family.

"I look training, but I don't know what I can do," Amna says.

Najma tells her about how much Dragon 360 has turned things around for her. She suggests to Amna that they could go and talk to Jonathan together tomorrow morning after drop off, about Amna joining the scheme.

The next day Jonathan greets Amna and Najma at Northside. He shows Amna the Dragon 360 portfolio document, reaching for the Urdu translated versions, and calling Mahnoor over to translate.

"We can offer you support to find out what you can do. It is all about life chances. Dragon 360 is run by the Welsh Government and it's free to everyone," he says confidently.

"But my English not very good," says Amna.

"Oh, we can help with that too as a part of the programme,“ says Jonathan. "We can offer you a 16 week English class with other people from the neighbourhood, as well as opportunities to practice your English, and you will get a certificate at the end of it."

Jonathan waits as Mahnoor translates.

"I know you've attended English classes here before Amna, and probably not been that impressed. But you'll both be pleased to know we've said goodbye to Mr Noakes, our former English teacher. He meant well but he really needed to go on some equality and diversity training. I still can't get over him doing pub role play during Ramadan!"

Amna is excited at the possibilities. She has seen that with some help, Najma has been able to turn her life around. Perhaps with the same assistance, she too can change her life chances.

SHE, Shireen and Desiree are meeting with the new Bristol mayor at his office. The local paper takes pictures of the four of them standing over an assemblage of their jewellery.

Life Chances have been personally invited by the Major to address the business leaders and councillors who have gathered to celebrate community business in the city.

SHE gives a speech about the women of Life Chances, their lives, and the obstacles and barriers they face. She has made the decision to enter the system, slightly, in order to change it from within.

"We had a meeting last night and we now have thirty members. We have come up with what we think is a strong manifesto – The Five Pathways to Community:

High value to be placed on the life of a human being;
High value to be placed on dignity, compassion, and respect for the humanity of another;
Security and opportunity for our children;

Freedom to celebrate ideas and culture;
Promoting mutual understanding rather than punishment.

So, there you have it. Life chances should be supportive, not punitive. We want to work with you, not for you or against you. And we want our new mayor to translate our manifesto into action," SHE says.

The gathered audience claps and more photographs are taken. People get up and examine the jewellery and exchange compliments with SHE and her friends.

The Mayor thanks Life Chances and follows up with his own speech:

"We intend to raise aspirations and tackle social isolation that people feel in our city. We want to bridge the gap between those people who are well off and those who are struggling to get themselves into a safe place. We know the government has a strong focus on life chances, but what we have just heard from these women is a real story, where they have taken a risk and shown people what they can do. We want to encourage more people to set out on a life chances agenda that is positive, creative and above all diverse and inclusive. I would like to thank them all personally, for showing us the way..."

Again the room claps and people begin to leave. SHE feels proud of what Life Chances has achieved. And this is only the beginning, she thinks, plenty more to come.

A voice whispers down the phone: "Hello, Barry, it's me, Toby."

"Toby, what the fuck are you doing, we've been fire-fighting a mess here now for three days, I need to speak to you urgently, you little..." shouts Barry.

"Meet me in the Q Park at Butler's Wharf near Tower Bridge in 15, I'll be in a white AC Cobra," Toby says.

"Toby, this is not some HBO thriller, you know, we have a real situation on our hands," shouts Barry. But Toby has hung up. Barry jumps out of his chair and orders Jane to get Harry round in the Bentley. That fucking little toe rag. Not only has Toby and his cohorts landed him in a pile of shit, but Barry also feels personally let down by Toby. He went out on a limb when he first hired Toby. He stuck with him, smoothing out some of his most anti-social behaviour and giving him free rein to exercise, it has to be said, his remarkable coding and logistical talents.

He tells Harry he'll drive himself and motors the Bentley the short distance down Upper Thames Street to the car park. He drives round until he sees the AC Cobra parked at one end of the car park. Toby jumps out and walks towards Barry.

"Barry, this thing is finished. I just wanted to let you know that *The Image* are all over this."

"You, Toby, have dropped me in the shit from a great height, I cannot believe you have gone against my trust so utterly and completely. And, yes Toby, we know that it was you that handed them the dossier of UC files. This is now in the hands of our lawyers and you will be hearing from us very soon."

"Look, I'm here in goodwill, Barry, I don't want hassle with you. But I can tell you that me and the orange guys have the keys to Deep Hole... What I'm saying Barry is, there's a situation where we hand over the 'reset' work all lovely bubbly like you want us to and there's another scenario where Deep Hole falls off a cliff. Do you get that, Barry?" Toby hunches his shoulders and sticks his hands in his pockets.

"Oh, yes, I get that Toby, I get that fine. What you're really saying is that you're blackmailing me. But I'm ahead of you Toby. I've already instructed all of the sysops people to lock you and your cronies out of the system."

"Yes, we know that, Barry, but would you expect the best IT team in the country not to build the odd back door or two? We have full administrator rights over the pilot systems all over the country. And we have installed some additional lines of codes in Agile 16.0."

Some of the colour starts to drain from Barry's face.

"Oh, I see. What will you be doing with KZM Closters then? Will they want a dodgy team of blackmailers working for them?"

"Actually, Barry, we will be taking on a big NHS contract with them and some upgrades for HMRC." Toby is clearly feeling very pleased with himself – he is acting like Walter White minus the pork pie hat and shades. And the methamphetamine. Barry realises he's got him cold.

"Alright, give us a proper hand-over and we'll take it from there," Barry sighs, caving in.

If he's lucky he'll get to hang onto his OBE and get a cushy number on the after dinner speakers circuit. The damage has been done and it's all about damage control now.

Toby nods, starts up the AC Cobra and screeches away. Barry thinks to himself that his life is becoming like an episode of *Breaking Bad*. Without the methamphetamine.

***The Image* goes to press** on the first part of the 'UC Dossier'. Early editions run out in Westminster, as the news works its way across the political village.

Diane produces a web version with a series of revelations about the handling of Universal Credit and the workings of G4N. There is a large picture of Barry Hamilton looking out over the Thames from his office.

Craig Tumbleton calls an Extraordinary General Meeting of the G4N board. Barry is hauled in front of them and asked to explain the situation.

"I apologise to the board. This was very badly handled by me, I take full responsibility for what has happened. We basically have a rogue individual and his department who have quite literally screwed us. I had no idea what was going on and I had no idea that this individual had access to all of these documents. I am willing to tender my resignation to you now and fall on my sword."

"I questioned your competency, Barry, last time," says Don Cox. "It turns out I was right." You're such a smug bastard, thinks Barry. The only reason Craig keeps you on the board, Coxy, is that you're his wife's godfather.

"Barry, you must have been aware that this individual was potentially trouble? Didn't this crop up in his HR continuing assessment?" asks Craig.

"No, it didn't – the individual did not attend any of his scheduled continuing assessment meetings with HR," says Barry.

"So, this didn't give you an alert or warning of some kind?" says

Baroness Sharmi Silver. Barry can see the Baroness is disappointed in him, which makes him feel worse. He always felt she understood him, but now she is blowing cold, just like old Coxy.

"It did.. But I knew he could actually fix Deep Hole and make it work. I still think he could but now they've all buggered off to KZM Closters to work on an NHS contract. So, we are shafted..."

"As Chair I am going to ask you to stay in post for a short time. I want you to see this through – when we've come out of the woods you will be tendering your resignation. I gather you are in line for an OBE, so I'm sure that will work its magic in ensuring your future employment," says Craig.

"Yes, thank you Craig and thank you to the board," says Barry.

Barry exits the board room and decides to go home. It's been a while since he fired up his train set in the attic and now feels like a good time.

Diane prepares the next item for the paper and checks in with Nick on the final copy.

"It's been brilliant, Diane, we have had so much traffic on this. The new government is already under pressure from us and the drip approach is working wonders. I have some news for you Diane too, we're going to offer you a Political Editor role with a permanent contract, what do you think? I know you've had an eye on my job for a while," says Nick.

Diane is taken aback by the offer and Nick's direct approach. "Well that's fantastic. And, well, you know it's nothing personal, I've just been looking for more stability. You know what it's like being a freelancer," Diane says, visibly blushing.

"I'm stepping up to Deputy Editor now that Sherry's gone to the *New Statesman*," says Nick, enjoying Diane's obvious discomfort. Not that he is bothered by her ambition. He was just the same when he was her age.

"So, will I get to commission as well as write?" asks Diane.

"Yep, you'll be in charge of a team of eight – two on the books and the others freelancers." says Nick. "Of course you'll still report to me."

"I wouldn't have it any other way," replies Diane. "That's until I become Editor, of course..."

The following day Diane's new piece appears in the paper. It tracks the muddles and waste of tax payer's money connected to Universal Credit.

In the afternoon, news comes over the Press Association wire that Ivan Dunhouse-Jones has resigned. Pictures of him start to appear in late editions of the *Evening Standard*. Head upright in the back of a Jaguar, Dunhouse-Jones looks straight ahead, not acknowledging the massed ranks of journalists desperately trying to get a quote.

Diane receives a phone call from a freelancer in her new office.

"Hi, my name's Hayley and I was wondering if you were interested in a series of articles on education? It's about the changes in the education system and how this affects people..."

"Hayley, to be honest, we have quite a few pieces on this at the moment and it needs to be distinctive for our readership," Diane says.

Hayley sounds dejected. Don't fall at the first hurdle, thinks Diane.

"I'll tell you what, I'll give you a bit of research time, that's what helped me, come and see me tomorrow afternoon for a chat," Diane says, feeling generous.

In her minds eye, Diane can see Hayley punching the air, but all she can hear on the phone is: "Yessss!"

Diane hangs up and looks at the drawing Samira, the young Somali asylum seeker she met in Bristol, gave her. A series of concentric circles radiate from the middle of the paper. Right in the middle of the circle Samira has drawn a flower, with tendrils connecting and breaking up the continuous hoops. She wanders where Samira and her mother are now. Of all the people she met on her tour of Britain, they seemed the most vulnerable. She picks up the phone again and calls Hayley. "There's something I'd like you to chase up for me..."

Barry sits at his desk looking over the barrage of reports on live contracts. He has to sign off at least four jobs by the end of the month and get the invoices out. He is now resigned to the fact that his days are numbered and he will be moving on.

He begins the process of building a new team for the 'reset' work in Universal Credit. After a series of interviews they decide to employ a new Chief Technology Officer, who has worked at the ministry, nothing fancy or risky this time.

Janice Robins starts work in the final few days of November. Her CV suggests that she is a safe pair of hands and she is. With a husband and kids at home, she works strictly timed hours, commutes in from East Croydon each day and always responds politely to internal requests.

Her first task is to assess where the reset work is up to and visit the pilot areas. She then secures the back-end from the previous orange team and tries to make sense of the roll-out work needed on Agile 16.0.

Barry gets rid of 'orange floor', replacing the pink sofas and bean bags with proper desks and chairs. Out go the vintage video games and retro vending machines. He has the bright red, blue and yellow of the walls repainted magnolia.

On 30th November, St Andrews Day, Janice holds a meeting to report back to Barry. The group of IT professionals cram into Barry's office and sit on the two settees. Barry pulls up another few chairs and is feeling jovial, having acquired an early demob happy feeling. Jane brings in tea for everyone and the meeting commences.

Janice speaks slowly and clearly to get her report across to everyone. She has a habit of letting her words enunciate too long, which Barry finds annoying. However, Barry is delighted that things are starting to calm down and he won't have to put up with Janice for much longer.

"We have spent the last fortnight gathering information on the pilot stages and we have some recommendations and a few quibbles. Of course we have secured everything as requested. We have also done as you asked and kept the DWP fully informed on where we are."

Janice stops and takes a sip of water.

"And, well, I...I had the team run test after test and I just can't explain it," Janice says looking nervous.

Oh god, thinks Barry, what now? "Well spit it out, whatever it is."

"Universal Credit, to the best of our knowledge, went live nationwide at 12 midnight last night. All the pilot stages are fully functional and the system is fit for purpose in all areas of the country."

There is a long silence, then,

"How the fuck did that happen?" asks Barry.